TO BE
AN ANCHOR
IN THE STORM

A Guide for
Families and Friends of
Abused Women

SUSAN BREWSTER, M.S.S.W.

Seal Press

Cover design by Clare Conrad
Cover photograph by PhotoDisc

Grateful acknowledgment is made to the National Coalition Against Domestic Violence, National Office, Denver, for permission to reprint their State Coalition Phone List.

Library of Congress Cataloging-in-Publication Data
Brewster, Susan.
   To be an anchor in the storm : a guide for families and friends of abused women / Susan Brewster.— 1st Seal Press ed.
      p.   cm.
   Originally published: New York : Ballantine Books, 1997.
   Includes bibliographical references.
   ISBN 1-58005-037-9
   1. Abused women—United States—Psychology. 2. Abused women—United States—Family relationships. 3. Abused women—Counseling of—United States. 4. Victims of family violence—United States. I. Title.
HV6626.2.B74 2000
362.82′92—dc21   00-035763
                                                                         CIP

Printed in Canada

Fonts: Weiss, Wade Sans Light, Type Embellishments

First Seal Press edition, May 2000

10   9   8   7   6   5   4   3   2   1

Distributed to the trade by Publishers Group West
In Canada: Publishers Group West Canada, Toronto, Ontario
In the U.K. and Europe: Airlift Book Distributors, Middlesex, England
In Australia: Banyan Tree Book Distributors, Kent Town, South Australia

AUTHOR'S NOTE

The cases described in this book are based on actual events. However, names and identifying characteristics have been changed to protect the personal privacy of those involved. Any resemblance to actual names or persons, living or dead, is thus purely coincidental.

This book contains the general opinions and advice of a licensed mental health professional concerning common domestic violence situations. Individual circumstances can vary widely, and an individual's circumstances may warrant seeking the help of qualified mental health, legal, or medical professionals. The author therefore encourages readers who are in dangerous or life-threatening situations to seek appropriate professional advice and assistance.

Contents

to R.M.B.

Introduction

It is estimated that up to four million women in the United States are beaten each year by their partners. Most of those women have at least one family member or friend who cares about them. That person may not know it, but he or she may be able to make the difference as to whether that woman resigns herself to a life filled with abuse or gains the sense of personal power she needs to make safe decisions and positive changes for herself.

IS THIS BOOK FOR YOU?

If you are reading this book, it is likely you are involved (as a relative or friend) with a woman whom you suspect or know is being physically or emotionally abused by her boyfriend or husband. You may have a disturbing sense that something is "wrong" in her relationship with her partner but you can't quite put your finger on what it is. You may be watching her life from a distance, safe from the gale yet engrossed in the drama, as if you were watching a ship tossed by a raging sea during a hurricane. You may be watching with guilty fascination, a voyeur to the chaotic events which seem to define their relationship. Or, you may be very close to her and be experiencing the waves of her feelings as if the abuse were happening to you. You may feel scared one moment because of the hostility which emanates from "him," but perfectly comfortable with him the next moment because he seems so normal. You may feel helpless because the police and courts can't stop him from hurting her. You may feel confused when she doesn't act logically. You may even be repelled by her inability to see in him what you see.

Most people in your situation have an urgent need to jump in, to intervene, to "fix it," because she doesn't seem to be able to fix it on her own. You may have already tried that, but to no avail. You may have come to a point where you don't know what to do.

WHO AM I?

I am a licensed psychotherapist with extensive experience working with battered women, their abusive partners, and families. I hold a bachelor's and a master's degree in social work and have worked in many different settings, counseling adults and children, over the last eighteen years. I've been a therapist at an outreach center for abused women, their partners, and children, and I've been the clinical director of a battered women's shelter. I have even had the opportunity to train police officers in responding to domestic violence calls.

I do not write this book simply from the viewpoint of a professional. I was also a battered woman, abused by a boyfriend I had many years ago. Fortunately, I was surrounded by supportive people, many of whom acted as anchors in different ways and at different times. Without those people my life would have progressed very differently, if it had been allowed to progress at all. I'm eternally indebted to each of them.

Though I have acquired the experience necessary to write this book, do I have the right to tell you what to do or how to be? If you were sitting in my office, I would not be giving you advice. That is not the way I do therapy. But a book is a one-way communication, and as such, I find I must be more "advising" in order to be helpful. I do keep in mind that families and individuals are all different. Strategies that work for some people may not work for others and flexibility is the key to mapping out any helpful plan. Indeed, I respect the right of anyone to choose to not make changes, to not become an anchor. Free choice is the basic tenet of positive and lasting change. It is important, though, that yours be informed choices rather than helpless reactions due to a lack of information or misinformation. To address this need I have put together, in this book, principles which have proven helpful to the friends and family members of abused women with whom I have worked.

JACKIE'S STORY

Jackie and I had been friends for three years before she first confided in me that her sister Diane was being battered by her husband. Though she knew, through those three years, that I had worked with battered women, she just didn't think to mention it. And, when she did mention it, it was almost in passing, as if she had never regarded the whole matter very seriously before. Jackie had never had a very close relationship with Diane and had never considered that there might be something she could do to help her.

Jackie had a lot of preconceived ideas about battering and battered women: they are stupid for staying, they can leave anytime they want, they are weak-willed, the abuse must not be too bad or they wouldn't be there, if an abused woman would just put her foot down the abuse would stop. These ideas effectively kept her from becoming involved with Diane. After we discussed spouse abuse issues which might apply to Diane's situation, such as the danger she might be in, the brainwashing she might be enduring, and the patterns involved in domestic violence, Jackie set out to educate herself. She read what she could find about battered women in the library and when I spoke with her after that, she had already begun to see Diane's situation in a different light.

Jackie came to realize how dangerous her sister's situation was and that she (Jackie) might be able to put herself in a position to make a real difference in Diane's life. Jackie and I worked together informally for the next eighteen months. Other friends and clients, before Jackie and since, have come to me for help with their battered loved ones and I will be telling some of their stories, as well as my own, to illustrate concepts I discuss. It was my experience with Jackie which spawned the idea for this book, and I follow her story throughout.

WHAT THIS BOOK IS ABOUT

This book is about testing your suspicions, choosing your role, and possibly reshaping your relationship with an abused woman you care about so that you can be of help. If what you suspect is true, you can be sure that her life is as tumultuous as a ship tossing helplessly in a gale, and as a ship needs safe anchorage, so does she. Although her actions won't always bear this out, a woman in an abusive relationship can be desperate for a solid base to turn to, an anchor to lend her perspective and nurture her self-esteem. This book will help you assess whether or not, and how, you might become that anchor for her. Other books about domestic violence or "intimate abuse" explain the dynamics involved, discuss treatment methods and give advice to battered victims or to batterers. This book seeks to explore the relationship between a battered woman and a concerned relative or friend. It is a hands-on, specific approach geared directly to your unique role.

Chances are that you have already had the desire to assist your abused friend or family member but have no idea how to do so; perhaps you have already tried and failed to be of help and want a new approach. For a battered woman, having an anchor can mean the difference between helplessness and empowerment to work toward a solution. You may decide you want to assume the role of anchor. Or, you may decide you are not willing or able to take on such a role. This book will explore with you the issues surrounding these decisions.

WHAT, THEN, IS AN ANCHOR?

The best way I have found to describe a helpful role for friends and relatives of battered women is to use the word "anchor." Picture yourself for a moment as an anchor sitting on the ocean floor. You are made of the strongest steel, able to resist the corrosive elements which surround you. You sit heavy and grounded, unwavering even under the strain of the tide. Attached by line to a ship, you serve to stabilize it, keeping it from going adrift. You are not there to control the ship. If a storm comes up, your line alternately tightens and loosens, giving leeway to the waves. Your job is to remain constant, never allowing too much slack. You don't go out and rescue your ship. Nor do you cut the line. Instead, you keep the line taut and the ship close, so it can always remember where it belongs in the sea.

An abused woman tends to be isolated, suspicious, fearful, and unpredictable. Being in a relationship with her is difficult. Those who care about her cannot ensure her safety, but in my experience, an abused woman who has an anchoring connection to someone outside her situation has a better chance of improving her life, a better chance of forging solutions. An anchor's unaggressive connection with an abused woman reminds her of her strength and fortifies her sense of herself. As an anchor, you are safe and sure in your instincts. You are stable and constant while she may be erratic and forgetful. You remember what she has told you and point out inconsistencies. She is reminded, through her dialogue with you, of her own depths, her own compromised safety system, her own neglected core. While there are no guarantees, an anchoring relationship increases the chances that the abused woman will begin to act on her own behalf.

Whether you are alone as helper, or share this connection with several, the principle under which you operate is the same.

The anchor analogy allows me to best describe the problems you might experience as well as the development you will probably undergo as a help or guide. As friend or kin, you may have reached a point where nothing you have tried so far works. You may feel that you are standing on the shore watching helplessly. But through a process of understanding and perhaps changing yourself, you can step into the sea and become an anchor to that floundering ship. Keep in mind that if your line is grabbed, the process of change for her may take months, years, or may not happen at all. An anchor is never in control of the ship. But your own transformation into an anchor brings with it unfathomable rewards. Jackie's story illustrates how, in bridging the distance between her and her sister, Jackie found inner strength and peace. Others would then seek her out as their anchor. And the ripples continue for her.

In this book I will show you a *way of being* with your relative or friend that fosters understanding on your part and trust on hers. I will show you how to shift from feeling powerless to being effectively involved. I will also explain the ins and outs of being of real help, of being an anchor. Anchor qualities can become a permanent part of you, a set of tools that you take out and use when you want or need them. As you develop these skills you will find yourself becoming a confidante; as you become more skillful, others may come to *you* with their stories.

WHAT IS PARTNER ABUSE?

Many people today are aware that partner abuse involves two adults who are in a personal relationship, but not necessarily married or even living together. They are also aware that the abuse often takes the form of an assault or bodily injury. However, many people are not as knowledgeable about the other acts associated with partner abuse. In New Mexico, where I live, the law regarding domestic abuse is quite progressive and clearly identifies the following acts committed by one person against another person between whom there is a continuing personal relationship as illegal: physical harm, severe emotional distress, bodily injury or assault, a threat causing imminent fear of bodily injury by any household member, criminal trespass, criminal damage to property, repeatedly driving by a residence or workplace, telephone harassment, stalking, or harassment.[1] Current New Mexico law reflects the growing recognition that domestic abuse is much more than a slap across the face.

Throughout this book I use the terms "abused woman" and "battered woman" interchangeably. Most physically abusive relationships begin with emotional abuse. Though some women undergo emotional but never physical abuse, I believe there is still a potential for physical abuse in most emotionally abusive relationships. Moreover, most women I've known who were "just" emotionally abused by their partners reacted to and felt similarly to women who were also physically abused. Granted, there is a difference between physical and emotional abuse. A woman who is emotionally abused fears for the loss of her self and sanity,

[1] Family Violence Protection Act, Section 40-13-2 NMSA 1978.

while a woman who is physically abused fears for the loss of her self, sanity, and life. This difference may seem rather unimportant, however, when you are considering becoming an anchor for an abused woman you care about. I believe the concepts contained within this book can be applied to anchoring a woman who is in either an emotionally or a physically abusive relationship.

HOW COMMON IS BATTERING?

The statistics can seem unbelievable. For instance, would you believe me if I told you that at least one out of seven women you know has been physically abused by a boyfriend or husband? It is statistically likely. A 1993 national poll found that 14 percent of American women (one out of seven women) acknowledged having been violently abused by a husband or boyfriend.[2] Even more troubling is that the actual number of abused women is probably much higher than statistical surveys reflect because women often don't report (to police or survey interviewers) the abuse they have experienced. In fact, intimate abuse remains one of the most underreported crimes.

The chances are great that you know a woman who has been battered in her lifetime. Chances are good that you have an acquaintance who is currently in a violent relationship. Perhaps there is even a woman you care deeply about who is in an abusive relationship right now. You may not realize she's battered because she keeps her secret well hidden. It is extremely embarrassing to admit

[2]Family Violence Prevention Fund, *Men Beating Women: Ending Domestic Violence, a Qualitative and Quantitative Study of Public Attitudes on Violence Against Women* (New York: conducted by EDK Associates, 1993).

to being battered. Many women don't even admit it to themselves.

THE POWER OF INFORMATION

You do not need to start out knowing much about the issues surrounding abused women in order to be helpful to an abused woman. I wrote this guide specifically to help you get started without being an expert. However, I do strongly believe in the power of information. Most people have preconceived notions about domestic violence which are often not based in fact. If you are open to new ideas, you are on your way to becoming more helpful. As you begin to use the new information, you will find yourself becoming more connected to the woman you care about. The more connected you are, the more trust she will develop in you. The more trust she has in you, the more likely she will be to seek your assistance. When she does seek your assistance, you will be better prepared to help her. This is the process of becoming her anchor. So, although the course is new and weather unpredictable, you can learn how to be an anchor. The information contained in this guide charts the way.

QUALIFICATIONS

I want to explain my use of the term "battered women" or "abused women." In describing the women who are the subjects of this book, I prefer "women who are battered/ abused" to "battered/abused women" because the latter has become a defining label with stereotypical connotations (that they are eternal victims, powerless in jobs and all relationships), rather than a way to describe an individual's circumstances. Despite my preference I have found it necessary to sometimes use "battered/abused women" for word economy. It is not meant to encourage or support a stereotypical image, of any sort, of women who are battered. For the same reasons I sometimes use the term "batterer/abuser" instead of my preference, "men who batter/abuse."

In this book I refer to batterers as being men and victims of intimate abuse as being women, because this represents the majority of cases with which I have had direct experience and also the majority of cases found in studies on U.S. demographics of domestic abuse. According to the U.S. Department of Justice, females annually experience over ten times as many incidents of violence by an intimate as do males.[3] It is in no way intended to discount the experiences of people who are victims of intimate abuse who don't necessarily fit into those configurations, such as male victims of abuse, teenage victims of dating violence, or victims of violence in same-sex relationships.

HOW TO USE THIS BOOK

This book is a guide designed to help you help an abused woman you care about. The first four chapters and Chapter Seven provide general information and explanations of relationship dynamics, preparing you to learn and utilize the anchor skills which are taught in Chapters Five, Six, and Eight. This book is not as cut-and-dried or sequential

---

[3]U.S. Department of Justice, Bureau of Justice Statistics, Selected Findings, "Violence between Intimates," November 1994. NCJ-149259.

as a how-to manual. To do the kind of work this book describes means that you will be involved in personal and interpersonal processes which can be complicated at times. Furthermore, your experience in doing this work will be different from every other person's, as your own unique personality and relationship style enters into it.

To get the most out of it, I suggest that you read the whole book through, taking it in as a whole before giving much time or conscious thought to any particular area. Through that first reading pay attention to the feelings and thoughts that pop into your mind. Maybe jot them down when they occur to you, but try not to analyze them.

At some point, let the book sit for a while and give the information time to jell. You will probably feel that you want to pick it up again. The next time you read it spend more time actively thinking about the information presented. You might notice that your mind has been working on it since you read it through the first time. You will know when the time is right to use the information contained in the book to help you determine where your relationship stands with the woman you care about and, then, what you can do to help her.

CHAPTER ONE

———— ∞ ————

To Care: Getting Past Suspicion and Myth

IT'S TOUGH TO BE YOU!

It can be very difficult to be a friend or relative of an abused woman. The more you care for her the more emotionally difficult it can be for you, even if you are not in contact with her. If you don't yet know for a fact that your loved one is abused but you suspect it, your relationship with her is probably strained. You might sense something is wrong in her relationship with her partner but don't have solid evidence that they're involved in something as stigmatizing as domestic violence. You might also find yourself feeling frustrated and confused by your loved one's behavior. You may notice that she tends to contradict herself and tells stories about her relationship that conflict with one another. One day she boasts that her partner is the most wonderful father, while the next she complains of his quick temper with the kids. One moment she tells you that no one has ever made her feel so special. Then she complains that he belittles her in front of his friends.

If you know for a fact that a woman whom you care about is being abused, it is probably bothering you at some level, whether or not you are admitting it to yourself. You might also find yourself confused. You may hear that he has stopped hitting her only to discover later that he is keeping her up arguing at night to the point where she is too exhausted to keep her job. Even more frustrating is that she may seem rather flighty herself. You might wonder how seriously you should take her hints about her partner's abuse if she can't hold a rational thought in her head, or hold a job, or keep her life in better order.

IT'S TOUGH TO BE HER!

Let's face it, an abused woman can seem, to the average person, pretty unstable! She can be forgetful, her thoughts scattered. Her behavior can be very erratic. She might seem depressed or ill-tempered, nervous or withdrawn. She might not follow through with things she plans to do, or keep promises. She might act as if she prefers to be left alone. Or, she might seem to be none of those things. She might come across as the epitome of emotional strength and personal success. Most likely, if you knew her before she met her abuser, she has gradually but significantly changed. At one time she may have been vibrant and lively; now she is lethargic and preoccupied. You may not understand why or how she got to be so out of balance. You just know that you don't like to be around her much anymore.

An abused woman leads a very precarious life. One

minute she is held out by her partner as the angel of his universe, while the next minute she's groveling at his feet like a whipped puppy, begging him to stop hitting her. One day he gives her flowers and a new car. The next day he stomps on the flowers and throws her car keys in the river. One week he does all the housework and takes the kids out so she can have some time alone. The next week he tells her that she's a sloppy housekeeper and a neglectful mother. One year (yes, there can be that much time between abusive incidents!) he's getting along with everyone at work and seems to be making friends. The next year he quits job after job and hangs out at the local bar getting in fights and losing grocery money on bets at the pool table. Is it any wonder that an abused woman becomes confused and depressed? Anyone would!

"SHE DESERVES WHAT SHE GETS" IF SHE STAYS

You might think that in some ways she causes her abuse. Many people involved in the life of a battered woman assume that, at the very least, she is responsible for deciding to stay with her partner after the abuse has begun. Statements I have heard from various people run the gamut: "I would leave a guy in a minute if he did that to me." "She must like it at some level or she wouldn't stay with him." "I have no sympathy for people who don't *do* something to change their situations." "There's no way she's battered, she's just as tough as he is." "But she's a lawyer! She's too smart to let some guy hurt her."

Perhaps you agree with some of these statements. If you do, you're not alone. In my experience most people hold some of these beliefs before they learn any facts about the issues surrounding domestic violence. Indeed, these are very common beliefs shared by people of many different backgrounds. I have even been shocked to hear a few of these statements made by members of my own family who knew about my own abuse experience! There are obviously some very pervasive beliefs about domestic abuse in our society, so pervasive that even victims of abuse sometimes believe them.

ABUSED WOMEN OFTEN DON'T KNOW WHY THEY STAY

Often, battered women are as confused as anyone about their own motives for staying with their abusive partner. Upon first entering counseling or a battered women's shelter, many women I have worked with have made statements like: "I must be crazy to still love him." "Why am I not strong enough to leave like other women that this happens to?" "I can't believe I'm going back to him after what he did to me this time." As a result of this confusion and self-blame, battered women often feel extremely ashamed and embarrassed. Then they become even *more* isolated and secretive, particularly with regard to those people who care about them most. Even if they do talk with friends or family about the abuse, they usually make it sound much less serious than it really is.

IT DOESN'T SOUND VERY DANGEROUS

Perhaps the woman you are concerned about doesn't make her relationship with her partner sound very bad;

therefore, you might assume it isn't. She describes her partner as having a "bad temper" or says that he gets "kind of crazy" at times. Or maybe she uses statements like "He blew up" or "He lost it" when she describes an argument with him. You might be thinking, doesn't everyone get mad sometimes and have arguments? Does that necessarily mean that there is physical abuse? And even if he pushes and shoves her a little during fights, does that automatically make someone a batterer? Anyway, all couples have problems, don't they? Troubled times pass. It isn't your business. Right? Besides, her behavior and his might seem so irrational that it begins to feel like you're watching a soap opera on television. You might decide that you have enough to worry about in your own life, that you don't need to be stressed out further with this continuous "melodrama."

IT IS *VERY* DANGEROUS

Still, you may have a nagging voice inside telling you that there could be more to this than meets the eye, that possibly you could help if you just knew how. This could really be dangerous for her, like the stories in the news in which a man stalks his ex-wife and kills her, or stories about a husband getting more cruel and torturous over the years and finally snapping one day, killing his family and then himself.

It is important for you to understand that YOU ARE PROBABLY ALLOWED TO SEE ONLY THE VERY TIP OF THE ICEBERG WHICH REPRESENTS HER ABUSIVE RELATIONSHIP. And what you do see is probably extremely skewed. When battered women choose to share information about their abuse with someone, they rarely present it in a complete and realistic way. They might minimize it to the extent that an all-day beating is presented as a minor "blowup." Nevertheless, despite the minimizations and distortions, it is possible to move yourself into a position where the woman you are concerned about shares enough for your suspicions to be confirmed or denied.

So, you can't necessarily gauge how seriously to take her situation by how she presents it, and even though you may only suspect that she is abused, the price of not confirming your suspicions is probably higher than you think. Are you prepared to sit back and do nothing when there may be a threat to her very existence? I'm writing to tell you, with all my conviction and experience, *her life is in danger* if she is in a battering relationship. She could die at the hands of this man who supposedly loves her.

YOUR CHALLENGE

If you are confused, imagine how confused *she* must be. If you still want to help, you can! But only if you are willing to unlearn the myths, unfeel some very natural feelings, and fight against some very basic instincts. In other words, you must change yourself!

But what if you're wrong and she's not in a battering relationship? Think about it. If you are wrong in your suspicions that she is being battered, and you apply the counsel of this book, you will have done no harm to her or anyone. You will, at the very least, have learned skills which could help you make closer emotional connections with other people in your life.

If you find that you are trying to break through the uncertainties and myths by searching for information about battering relationships, give yourself a lot of credit. You have already begun the learning process that will most likely cause you to question some of the beliefs you have now. It can be a humbling experience to find out that what you once assumed to be right about her situation is wrong. The important thing is that you are motivated to learn in order to be of real help to her, to become her anchor. That is probably why you picked up this book. The biggest challenge in this process is that it will require you to make some personal changes, perhaps some very deep personal changes.

CHAPTER TWO

————∞∞∞————

Realizing the Distance
You Must Bridge

Without your abused relative or friend's trust, you can neither determine the real nature of her predicament nor select ways to be of help. This chapter will help you assess the gap you must close.

If you were close to her before she became involved with her abusive partner, you may notice that the emotional distance between the two of you has widened. WHEN ABUSE BEGINS IN A WOMAN'S RELATIONSHIP, HER OTHER RELATIONSHIPS CHANGE. And, rather than becoming closer, as one would hope, those relationships often grow more estranged. What happens to create a split between a battered woman and those who care about her is very complex. But such a split is important for you to understand as a starting point, so that you can counteract the feelings and behaviors which cause the emotional distance.

On the other hand, your relationship with your friend

or relative may be completely estranged—you are an anchor sitting in a harbor shop and she's a ship hundreds of miles out to sea. You may never have been particularly close to her and feel even farther from her since she became involved with him. Alternatively, you may see her every day and talk with her about every subject under the sun except her partner's violent behavior—you are near and available, an anchor grounded solidly on the ocean bottom, but she is a ship tossing helplessly about on the waves above you, reluctant to tie up to you.

IT IS IN YOUR POWER TO ALTER YOUR RELATIONSHIP WITH YOUR FRIEND OR LOVED ONE. In effect, by discarding your "script," by resisting your natural and predictable reaction to something she has done or said, and by becoming the initiator, you change the pattern. You send important signals: I'm safe to talk to and I'm available to help. Risking rejection, you open yourself up to her in the hope that she will eventually reciprocate your efforts toward closeness. For example, if you have always called her for a specific reason, by calling her just to catch up, you will be changing your pattern of behavior. She might for the first time realize that what you care about most is her, and not some agenda you have.

A MUTUAL CONNECTION MUST BE ESTABLISHED BEFORE SHE WILL TRUST YOU ENOUGH TO SEEK YOU OUT AS HER ANCHOR. In the following sections I outline some typical attitudes and behaviors (hers and yours) which can become barrier reefs standing in the way of that connection being developed. Later in this chapter I will step back and show you how these individual reefs create an ever-widening overall dynamic. Once you see the big picture you will be surprised to see how you can tinker with it and establish a new grounding of trust.

HER DISTANCE

The attitudes and behaviors discussed in this section have the effect of sealing off an abused woman from those who might help. Some are intentional, but many are inadvertent and not to be taken personally. Knowing about her possible motivations and point of view can help you empathize with her, put you in her shoes. By looking at her side you are mapping a course around the menacing reef which stands between you, an important first step in successfully navigating that reef.

HER MINIMIZATION

I have sat before women with swollen faces, bloodshot eyes, and bruised bodies who say without irony, "We had another argument and I got pushed around a little." Later, perhaps after they had been away from their partners and safe for a while, I would hear a much different and more appalling rendition of the same incident. As I came to know the particular woman's situation better, the second story usually proved to be the more accurate version.

BATTERED WOMEN USUALLY MINIMIZE THE EXTENT TO WHICH THEY ARE ABUSED. In other words, when they do tell someone about how their partner hurts them, they often make it sound much less serious than it really is. Some women do this by using palatable words to describe the violent acts perpetrated against them. Others leave out significant details about the incident. Many women will provide only carefully edited snippets of information which make less of an impact on the listener than if the whole story were told.

Battered women need to minimize the extent of the violence for many reasons which vary from individual to individual. Many battered women minimize because they are EMBARRASSED. They feel foolish for "letting this happen" to them. Before they found themselves loving a batterer, they believed they would never be with a man who treated them badly. They believed women who "put up with a guy like that" were stupid. When they wake up with a bruised face, courtesy of their partner, they feel very ignorant and ashamed. Moreover, they fear the condescending reactions of others, statements like, "Why do you stay with a guy like that? I'd never let anyone lay a hand on me!" Minimizing helps a woman who is battered avoid facing the judgments of others and herself.

Sometimes battered women minimize because they feel RESPONSIBLE for their partner's abusive behavior, or responsible for their relationship going awry. Most battered women search their memories for something they might have done or not done to cause his violent behavior. Some women actually *hope* they are responsible so that, by changing their own behavior, they can keep him from being violent again. They search desperately for control, a way to keep their relationship intact and yet safe.

What's more, batterers help those women feel responsible by maintaining that their violence toward their partners is justified: "If she would just keep the house clean like I asked I wouldn't have to *teach her a lesson*," or "If she wouldn't keep nagging at me I wouldn't have to lose my temper with her the way I do." Many people in our society also believe that battered women are in some way responsible for the beatings they endure: "What did she do to *make him* so mad?" To save face, some women respond to this societal blame by minimizing the extent of the abuse: "If people learn how violent he really is they are going to think I must be a real bitch to cause him to act this way."

In some cases women minimize because they are CON-CERNED that the people who care about them might not be able to handle the truth, they might worry incessantly, become violent themselves, or fall apart emotionally. Many an abused woman has told me that she didn't tell her family or friends of her predicament because they "have enough problems of their own, they don't need mine."

Related to this, a battered woman sometimes worries that if family or friends knew how dangerous her partner really was, those people would attempt to control her. It's probably all she can do to handle her partner's overcontrol and overreactions, she doesn't have the energy to handle that from anyone else. So she might minimize to keep that from happening.

Many women minimize the abuse they endure to PRO-TECT their partners. It is natural to want to protect the one you love and, as hard as it may be for you to understand, many battered women feel love for their partners. Most batterers can act very lovable. They can be very attentive, generous, and tender. A batterer will often present himself as a gentle but misunderstood man who just needs a part-ner's true love to bring out his potential. As a result of this facade, a battered woman may describe her abusive partner as "a really good person underneath who just needs my love and appreciation." She may feel the need to protect him from those people who don't seem to see in him the quali-ties she sees.

A woman may want so badly for her relationship to work that she keeps herself from having any thoughts or hearing any suggestion that it might not work. She pre-sents her partner in the best possible light so as not to have to hear what others might say about him and his abusive behavior. Anyone who does talk badly about him, or even agrees with her if she speaks badly of him, can expect her to eventually come to her partner's defense.

Most women minimize to some extent because they FEAR what their partners will do to them should they tell people the truth. A batterer is usually very clear to his partner that he wants her to keep quiet about the abuse, "or else." She knows only too well what "or else" means.

Batterers are afraid for their partners to have an emotional relationship with anyone but them. There is rarely room for more than the batterer in a battered woman's life. She must constantly juggle his need to possess and control her with her own need for emotional connections with others. If one of those others is you, expect that as you and she grow more connected, strange things will begin to happen which are designed to impede that developing closeness. Her partner may throw up obstacles to your establishing a closer relationship with her. For example, he might get sick and need her to stay home with him every time she has made plans to go out with you. Or, he might talk badly about you and belittle her for spending time with you.

She may distance herself from you when your relationship begins to cause conflict in her relationship with her partner. For example, she might start arguments with you over trivial matters so that you won't want to spend time with her. Or perhaps she makes up elaborate stories about why she can't spend much time with you anymore.

Another reason a battered woman might minimize is that her partner probably minimizes the extent of his violence. A batterer usually presents an incident as much less severe than it really was. He might even claim that it didn't occur at all or that he doesn't remember it happening. He can be so convincing that his version of the abuse incident is frequently believed by outsiders (even supposedly knowledgeable outsiders) above hers. He might even accuse his victim of being hysterical if she presents the abuse as it really occurred. He can make it look as if she is so overly emotional that she exaggerates the stories of marital discord. Indeed, he can be so persuasive that she, already worn down, may begin to believe him and disbelieve herself, reducing his treatment of her to just a "communication problem" like every other couple has from time to time.

Regardless of how or why the minimized stories develop, some battered women begin to believe their own minimized versions. A self-protective process begins whereby the woman gradually detaches her mind from her body. Her body cries out in pain and knows it has been violated, but her mind begins to respond, "No, it really isn't that bad. Ignore it."

HER IGNORANCE AND DENIAL

MINIMIZATION PAVES THE WAY FOR A BATTERED WOMAN TO DENY THE REALITY THAT THE MAN SHE LOVES, IN WHOM SHE IS DEEPLY INVESTED, IS CAPABLE OF SERIOUSLY HURTING OR KILLING HER. Initially, it is as hard for her to grasp that grim reality as it is for those who care about her.

During the early phases of an abusive relationship a battered woman often doesn't view her partner's behavior toward her as abuse or even violence. She is not likely to agree with you if you define it using those words. She probably won't view her situation as bad enough to warrant those labels, and she certainly won't believe he's capable of killing her. If she believed that, she wouldn't be with him.

After several very dangerous incidents, a battered woman might begin to realize that her partner is capable of seriously hurting or even killing her while she's in the relationship. But by then she also believes (because he has promised her) that he will hurt or kill her if she leaves him. So she becomes caught in a catch-22. If she leaves or even seeks help from someone and her partner finds out about it, she will face his wrath. If she doesn't leave, she is stuck in an abusive relationship which typically gets more violent with the passage of time. In addition to the danger, leaving may pose extreme financial, social, and emotional hardships. On the other hand, staying is most likely economically and emotionally difficult, too. There appears to be no good choice and it seems that she will lose either way. Facing this conflict is extremely painful. It can be easier in the short run to deny that her partner is dangerous to her, thereby circumventing the whole awful dilemma.

So, once a battered woman faces the truth about her partner's violent nature, she must also face the real threat he is to her and then make hard choices about her safety and future with him. It's much easier in the short run to minimize or completely deny his abuse to herself and others. To deny his abuse makes staying with the batterer more sustainable.

Some women hang on to their denial for many years. Others seem to work through the process of realization rather quickly. Many variables exist which influence how long a woman might hold on to denial, but an anchor's support is one thing that can move that process along.

A woman experiencing emotional abuse finds it particularly difficult to recognize the pain that she endures and to label it abuse. Emotionally abused women have told me that they wished they had physical evidence of the psychological scars their partners leave when they call them names, criticize or belittle them, or otherwise consistently undermine their power. It happens so subtly, they tell me, that they can't put their finger on what is happening to them until it's too late, they've already begun to internalize the negative comments and feel vaguely depressed and to blame for problems in their relationships. An emotionally abused woman doesn't have a bruise to point to and say clearly, he did this to me.

Many battered woman appear to be in denial about the abuse when really they are simply ignorant of the facts surrounding domestic violence. Battered women can be as ignorant to those facts as anyone else. For example, most battered women I worked with initially came into counseling believing that their partners' violent behavior toward them was a temporary, situational problem. They believed their partner was reacting to stress at work or home and that once the stress was alleviated, the beatings would stop. These women were coming to counseling to find out how to eliminate the stress from their partners' lives. The first few counseling sessions consisted mostly of teaching them the dynamics of physical violence within a relationship. When they learned that the cause of violent behavior was within the batterer, that batterers share similar characteristics, and that there is a pattern to the violence (see Chapter Seven for more on batterers), many women began looking at their relationship and situation much more objectively. Some women still dismissed the information I supplied as applying only to others' relationships, not their own.

To review, the battered woman you care about is likely to minimize the extent of physical abuse perpetrated against her for a variety of reasons: because she might feel embarrassed, responsible for her abuse, defensive, afraid, concerned about others' reactions, ignorant of the facts, or so dissociated from her pain that she has come to believe the minimized stories.

If she does minimize the extent of his violence or completely denies that he is dangerous to her, the situation is ripe for misunderstanding by people outside the abusive relationship, like you. And, with this degree of misunderstanding, isolation from friends and relatives is inevitable.

HER PHYSICAL DISTANCE

Physical distance is another way battered women become emotionally separated from those people who care about them. Batterers usually instigate this distancing method. They subtly or directly work at isolating their partner from those who might act as anchors for her. It is in a batterer's best interest for his partner to have no anchor; in case she decides to leave him she will have no one to help her make decisions or locate a safe place to stay. For her to be physically as well as emotionally isolated paves the way for him to escalate his use of control and violence within their relationship.

How is this physical distance created? Often batterers simply inform their partners that they are going to move to another city or state far from home (away from *her* friends and family). He might present his decision to his partner in a very positive way: "We're going to have it a lot better there financially." Or, he may be more negative: "You need to grow up and get away from your meddling relatives." In a more subtle way, he might create distance by not paying phone bills so the phone service is cut off, or by withholding her mail from her.

Batterers, however, are not always the instigators of physical distance. A battered woman sometimes initiates a move away from familiar surroundings with the hope that her abusive partner will be less "stressed" in the new place. For example, she might have phone service disconnected presuming that, without phone calls, her partner won't have cause to be so jealous, accusing every caller of being a secret boyfriend.

An abused woman creates and sustains physical distance from family and friends, hoping that things will get better in her relationship with her partner. What she may not realize is, A BATTERER IS USUALLY MORE LIKELY TO BE ABUSIVE TO HIS PARTNER IF SHE IS PHYSICALLY DISTANT FROM THOSE WHO CARE ABOUT HER. If she cannot readily get to her anchors and support systems, she is actually in more danger from his abuse, not less! Furthermore, her physical distance may have caused such emotional distance, she may not even have anchors or support systems left to go to. If she has nowhere to go and no one to turn to her partner is freer to abuse her without concern about her leaving the relationship.

YOUR DISTANCE

Family members and friends can also have preconceived ideas and feelings which create largely unintended distance from the abused women they care about.

HEARING HER

You as a relative or friend of a battered woman may be the first to suspect that your loved one is being battered, but the last to literally hear that it is happening. Battered women are usually very careful not to disclose the abuse to anyone but their most trustworthy anchors. Yet even if she does inform you of the abuse, your own guilt, anger, or shame (to be discussed later in this section) can keep you from comprehending her words. You might dutifully listen any time she talks, but you may inadvertently close your mind to the meanings to which she alludes, or you might be asking questions which tend to shut down a conversation rather than open it up. For example, she might casually mention to you that her husband is very jealous (e.g., "Whenever I go anywhere without my husband he accuses me of going there to meet another man"). What you choose to do with that disclosure will determine which message she receives from you. You can nod and let her comment stand, which might be the most comfortable option for you, but gives her the message that you don't want to know more about the subject. Or, you can ask her what she meant by her comment (e.g., "What do you mean, jealous?"). This option invites her to share more with you. This is all to say that you will be of most help to her if you assume there is *much more to understand* and she is revealing only the tip of the iceberg.

OBSTACLES TO HEARING HER

There are many possible reasons for the "communication gap" between a battered woman and her loved ones. Sometimes her loved ones don't really want to know the truth. It's too painful or confusing; after all, if they knew more, what on earth would they do or say? Some will be forced to look harder at their own attitudes and relationship difficulties if they hear her story of abuse. Many will have to change their preconceptions about domestic violence if they open their minds enough to really hear. So, at a basic level, to really hear her story forces the listener to deal with his or her own uncomfortable feelings.

Surprisingly, your own guilt may be holding you back

from connecting with her. Many parents, in particular, feel that their daughter's choice of a partner is, in some part, their fault—if they had been better parents their daughter would have chosen a "healthier" man. Or, the secrecy and denial surrounding domestic violence in our society can cause you to feel shame ("This can't be happening in a nice family like ours"). Because of this guilt and shame, it's easy for family members to not want to believe the abuse is happening, and to effectively shut their ears and close their eyes to the clues which might exist.

You may feel ANGRY at the battered woman you know, and your anger may be keeping you from getting closer to her. It's hard to see a woman you care about experience great anguish after a beating, only to watch helplessly while she excitedly returns to the man who beat her. Many friends and family members end up washing their hands of her after several of these cycles. They don't want to hear about it or talk about it anymore because it has become too painful and frustrating.

You may feel angry because your battered friend or relative is unusually needy or clingy. She may come to you time and again for advice on what to do about her relationship, only to do just the opposite of what you suggest. Or, she might accept your advice and use your help but never seem to make progress toward her own independence. You might even find yourself making up reasons to be less available to her in an attempt to handle your anger at her neediness.

She may, on the other hand, make it clear that she couldn't care less about your opinion or advice about her relationship with him. This can make anyone mad. You might be angry that she is breaking up her marriage. Perhaps you feel that divorce is unacceptable under any circumstances, that if they both tried harder they could work it out.

Anger can be rooted in past issues between you that are dredged up by the current situation. For example, if you have always been frustrated by her stubbornness, you may now find yourself particularly angry when she insists upon staying with her abusive husband. If you have always worried about her passivity, you might now feel angry about her unwillingness to "stand up to him" and fight back.

You may even have a strongly negative, almost sick, feeling in the pit of your stomach when you think of her. If you find yourself REPULSED by the thought of her or her circumstances, you could be headed for a lot of hard work toward bridging the distance between the two of you. I believe that when people feel as strong an emotion as repulsion toward someone, it usually has some root with that person's own experience. For example, a man who watched his mother being abused by his father when he was a child might feel repulsed when his daughter marries a man who abuses her.

Try to determine if your negative feelings toward her, whether they be anger, repulsion, or other negative feelings, are more about your own or past issues rather than about her abuse experience. If you put forth the effort it takes to work out those issues, you will free up energy to help her with her current problems.

YOUR MINIMIZATION

Inaccurate BELIEFS about intimate abuse can cause you to act toward her in such a way as to create distance. Beliefs have a sneaky way of becoming actions which you may not have consciously intended. You may believe, for instance, that spouse abuse is like scenes in some older movies, where a husband passionately slaps his wife's face in order to calm her down. Our media (television, magazines, movies) frequently promote false ideas about what really happens in abusive relationships. One example of this is the popular TV show from the 1950s, *The Honeymooners*. A cornerstone of the humor in this show was Jackie Gleason's character Ralph Cramden's frequent statement to his wife, "to the moon," as he mimicked with his hand her flying away after being hit.

While the media has become better about presenting the realities of domestic violence, inaccuracies still exist and these may have influenced your ideas or opinions about what your friend or family member is experiencing. If a woman you care about comes to you and says that her husband hit her last night, and you believe that the Hollywood view of spouse abuse is accurate, you may assume that the abuse she endured is not very dangerous. If you did that, you would be minimizing the extent of her abuse experience and probably alienating her from you. She is not likely to come back to you for help or support if you don't give her the respect to try to understand what *her* experience is or was.

YOUR ROLE AS ANCHOR IS TO MAKE YOURSELF READY TO HEAR HER. Intimate abuse is emotional and physical abuse of a very serious nature. It never stops with one beating. Both you and she will be on a journey to face that truth if you can listen to and be open with each other.

YOUR IGNORANCE AND DENIAL

One of my close relatives, who was aware of the abuse I had experienced, recently told me of a coworker who had asked her if she knew anyone who had been battered. She had replied to her coworker that she did not. Even as she was retelling the story to me she neglected to recognize that she did, indeed, know someone who had been abused—me! When I called her attention to that fact she said that she didn't think of me as being in the same category as all "those other" battered women. I was somehow, in her mind, different.

Like many other people, you may BELIEVE that domestic violence occurs only in other families or, at least, "not in my neighborhood." You may believe this simply because you are ignorant of the facts surrounding the problem. However, you may persist in thinking that intimate abuse occurs rarely or only in certain types of homes, even when you have been presented with information to the contrary. If you fail to reevaluate the validity of your beliefs even when presented with adequate information which disputes them, you may be denying the reality of the problem.

When I worked as a counselor in a suburb of a metropolitan area, we, at our center, encouraged a community organization from a neighboring upper-middle-class suburb to work with us to provide outreach services to battered women in their area. We were politely informed that *there were no battered women there.* We informed them that we knew there were battered women who lived in their area because we were receiving calls from them. They politely reiterated that they didn't need services for battered women and refused our help. Their community had closed its ears to the screams of the battered women who lived there. Theirs might have been either a lack of awareness or a denial of the problem, we never knew which. It was maddening to us at the time but it illustrates what many relatives and friends believe—this just doesn't happen to *our* kind of people. It also suggests that friends and relatives may be looked down upon by people in a community if it becomes known that a woman who is close to them is battered; they may feel ashamed or be shamed by others in their community. That may be the price of some truth.

JUST AS IT IS PARTICULARLY DIFFICULT FOR EMOTIONALLY ABUSED WOMEN TO RECOGNIZE THE PAIN OF THEIR EXPERIENCE, IT IS ALSO DIFFICULT FOR FRIENDS AND FAMILY MEMBERS TO RECOGNIZE THAT EMOTIONAL ABUSE IS TRULY ABUSE. One friend of mine who was emotionally abused in her first marriage tells a story of trying to explain to her mother how her husband hurt her with words, and restrictive and punitive rules. Her mother's reaction was, "At least he doesn't hit you. Maybe if you join a bowling league things will look up." Her mother's ignorance and denial about emotional abuse only validated my friend's self-doubt and lack of awareness of her own experience. It was many years before she came to recognize the extent of her own suffering. When she did, she divorced her husband and began working on what she had control of, her own life.

If you are ignorant of the facts or deny that domestic violence is a problem in your area and that it could happen to someone you know, you will inevitably create distance between yourself and a friend or relative who might be being abused. Your ignorance or denial will show itself to her in one way or another, whether it's a comment about her abuse (e.g., "You don't seem like the type to be in an abusive relationship") or an offhand comment regarding abuse in general (e.g., "Abused women are crazy"). If she does discover you are ignorant or in denial she will either find someone else with whom to share it, someone who is more open to learning about *her* experience, or worse, keep her secret to herself.

OVERCONTROL

If you find yourself constantly worrying about your loved one's problems or hastily putting together plans on what actions she should take, you may have a tendency to overcontrol her. I've seen family members and friends overcontrol a battered woman in many ways. Most people control subtly: "We'll buy you a car if you move in with us (and away from him)"; but some are quite direct: "If you don't file charges against him we will arrange it so that no one in the family will baby-sit for you." Suffice it to say that you are attempting to take too much control over her life if you, and not her, are the one consistently directing or controlling plans of action *on her behalf*. You may do it out of feelings of love, hopefulness, helplessness, or disdain, but the effect is still greater distance between you.

Overcontrol creates distance in several different ways. From infancy people have an innate and very strong need to control themselves and their surroundings. They also have a strong need to make connections with other people, to get love. Abused women are no different. If an abused woman feels that you are trying to control her life in some way, she is likely to either distance herself from you in an angry attempt to take back control over her life, or allow you to control her life in a passive attempt to minimize conflict between you, to stay connected to you. Whichever way she responds, she does not gain a sense of her own power to make decisions and changes in her life. If she reacts passively you are likely to feel justified in your control of her and you may even increase control over her: "She wants and needs my help worse than I thought." If she reacts with distance you are likely to emotionally distance yourself out of your own feelings of anger and frustration: "Why should I continue to be there to help her? She clearly doesn't want my help with her problems." Either way, neither of you wins.

JACKIE'S DISTANCE FROM DIANE

Remember Jackie, whose experience becoming an anchor for her sister Diane spawned the idea for this book? When she began her anchor work she was both physically and emotionally distant from Diane. Diane lived in another state and they had never been close as sisters. Jackie had great distance to conquer, but she also had tenacity.

When Jackie first talked to me about her sister, she knew for a fact that Diane was in a physically abusive marriage. That information, however, had a way of not registering in her brain. It went in one ear and out the other.

Jackie didn't hear about Diane's abuse for several reasons. She believed that Diane, like all battered women, was weak and stupid for staying with her husband; also, if she "didn't like it she wouldn't stay." Related to this was Jackie's belief that Diane would leave her husband if she just had enough willpower. Jackie had always been able to will herself into achieving her own goals, so she assumed Diane should be able to do that, too. Ignorant of the facts surrounding domestic violence, Jackie bought Diane's minimizations of the abuse and didn't think her situation was very dangerous. To Jackie, it didn't seem like abuse at all; rather it seemed like any other chaotic, dysfunctional marriage. Neither Diane nor anyone else challenged Jackie's prejudices.

Through her talks with me and her own reading, Jackie began to recognize how much distance there was between her and Diane, but she didn't know who had initiated it, when it began, or why. She eventually came to the awareness that they had become distant long before Diane had entered into an abusive marriage. Still, Jackie lacked the motivation to become an anchor until she opened her mind to new information regarding domestic violence and her relationship with her sister. The information she received frightened and appalled her so much that she was motivated to immediately address her own part in the distance, for the sake of herself and her sister. And so she embarked on her journey toward becoming Diane's anchor.

THE "GAP"

As you can see, there are often intense feelings between a battered woman and her family and friends. Just as you may be feeling guilty, angry, helpless, or repulsed, the abused woman may be feeling embarrassed, afraid, defensive, responsible, or concerned about you. When one person in a relationship separates him- or herself emotionally or moves in too close, the other person reacts, often by either retreating or moving in closer. It can become a relentless cycle with each person reacting to the other's reaction . . .

She minimizes, so you minimize, so she feels hopeless, so she is needy, so you overcontrol, so she feels worthless, so she denies there is abuse, so you feel helpless, so you distance physically and don't listen effectively to her, so she physically distances, so you feel hopeless and distance even further.

. . . resulting in a communication gap between people where there might have once been none.

THE "ARMS RACE"

Most people know only too well about the Cold War and the arms race between the old Soviet Union and United States, two superpowers reacting to one another in an ever-expanding buildup of weaponry and hostilities. The same process can happen between an abused woman and her potential anchors when communication breaks down.

Several things occur as communication between two people begins to deteriorate. First, we assume rather than ask. I assume either a motive that is convenient (fortifies my beliefs, protects my safe view of the world) or I assume the worst (that you are hostile, the enemy, the carrier of my worst fears). Trust breaks down and we make an internal, often automatic decision to arm ourselves. Once this defensive pattern begins, the parties are no longer themselves. They *become* their defenses.

Each party puts on more and more armor. Soon, all that each of them can see is the armor, not the real person beneath it. I am reacting not to you, but to your defenses, so I become more defensive. I begin with my chain mail, you react by putting on yours. I then slip on a breastplate, you add yours. I grab my shield and you react to my increased defensiveness by increasing your own. Each of us either reacts in kind or ups the ante. Now we have layers of metal and weaponry and distance between us. We are reacting to each other's reaction, seemingly locked in a contest whose rules are simple and primitive: survival! We've lost our common ground. We cannot work together toward any common purpose because our actions are limited to defense—we're too busy defending ourselves and countering the other's maneuvers. It's a primitive reflex action. We're reduced to survival, rather than the pursuit of happiness.

But hurt and confusion bring another factor into play: escalation. To escape my pain I must push you away and protect myself. To push you away I might decide to up the ante by bringing out a more advanced weaponry than what you're using. The Cold War has begun—like two hostile countries we don't know one another anymore, we only know one another's defenses. Because of our distrust, we can no longer interact, we can only react.

How do we end the race, stop the escalation? How do I find out who you are, underneath those primitive survival reflexes? How do you see beneath my armor? One of us has to take a risk and take off some armor. I must give you an opening, take off my breastplate. You might misread my initial move to remove my armor as a threatening gesture and deliver a fatal blow. The person who takes the first step must use the element of surprise—either do nothing to defend or do something conciliatory.

HOW CAN YOU STOP THE ARMS RACE?

The misunderstanding and distance which results when a relationship becomes engaged in an arms race can cause great damage to that relationship. That damage must be repaired before trust will develop.

Relationships are multifaceted entities, and, as such, no one person is to blame for the distancing problems which exist within a given relationship. For the same reason, no one person can solve all of those problems. However, one person can begin the process of change in the hope that the other person will pick up the other end of the rope.

The kind of work I am proposing in this book is such that you can begin forging yourself as anchor without her participation, if need be. You can try to identify your own part of this complex pattern. Then you can make a plan, using the next few chapters as a guide, for a closer connection. If you turn yourself into a strong anchor and remain tied to your buoy, beckoning where she can see it, she is likely to eventually attach herself to you. YOUR SUCCESS IS NOT CONNECTED TO WHETHER OR NOT SHE LEAVES HER ABUSIVE PARTNER. You will be successful when you achieve a stronger emotional connection with her.

You can decide to intercede at any point that you find yourself involved in an arms race with the woman you care about. Without her active involvement or even awareness, you can stop the downward spiral of hostilities or indifference by the way you react to her. You can act in such a way that will shift the course of the whole interaction toward a more positive and intimate exchange. The race cannot continue if you refuse to be a part of it. You can, instead, act like an anchor. Throw down your arms, lower your defenses, and show her that you are safe to talk to. Maybe then she will do the same.

THE ARMS RACE IN REAL LIFE

Sisters **JACKIE** and **DIANE** had been engaged in their own form of the arms race since they were children. Having never considered each other as playmates when they were young, they grew into adults who rarely considered each other at all, much less as friends. The less they talked, the greater the gap between them. With little to connect them emotionally, their misperceptions about each other grew as the years passed. To Jackie, Diane seemed like a submissive doormat for men, with no goals of her own. To Diane, Jackie seemed like a stuck-up, bossy oldest sister who had her own life in perfect order at all times. They each focused solely on that which confirmed those perceptions, closing their eyes to anything that contradicted them. Jackie failed to consider how hardworking and goal-oriented Diane was, always holding down steady jobs despite the constant stress she endured at home. Diane failed to recognize that Jackie had a soft side, a part that needed people and wasn't as perfect as she presented. As their misperceptions hardened, so too did their defenses, as each closed off parts of her life to the other's view. As a result, they each felt subtly attacked, which in turn produced the need to defend themselves with greater distance. Ironically, it was that distance which fostered the misperceptions and was therefore at the root of the unspoken hostilities between them. When Jackie realized this and made a conscious decision to lay down her arms, calling Diane and talking in a nonjudgmental way, Diane responded in kind. She had no more need to defend herself. She was safe to put down her own arms and open up to Jackie in a way she never had before.

JOSIE, a client of mine who was in an abusive relationship, mustered the courage to tell her parents parts of her story. Because they believed battered women were from "low-class" families, they assumed that their daughter, being from an "upper-class" family, would never be in an abusive relationship. So they were not able to hear her when she tried to tell them how her boyfriend had hurt her. They continually shifted the focus of the conversation toward more comfortable topics.

Josie assumed, from her parents' reaction to what she chose to tell them, that her secrets were too abhorrent for them to handle. To soften the impact on them, she minimized the extent of the abuse, painting a rosier picture than really existed. She would tell them that her boyfriend was a little "hot-tempered" and that he tended to "make a big deal about nothing." She decided to keep most of the truth to herself and further isolated herself from relatives so as not to be "found out." Josie's partner had been encouraging her distance from her parents anyway, so, she figured, increased distance would probably make him feel less tense.

Josie's parents saw her pulling away but didn't understand why. They assumed that she didn't want their help with whatever problems she was dealing with and began to distance themselves, to ease their feelings of helplessness and confusion. This made it easier for Josie to isolate herself further. Her partner's abuse worsened as she had fewer options and potential anchors. When she was finally ready to leave her boyfriend, it seemed to her that she had no one left to turn to for help.

Josie's experience illustrates how easily family members' preconceived ideas about abuse and their subsequent feelings can result in misunderstandings, false assumptions, and ultimately in greater emotional distance. Had either Josie or her parents reacted to the other a little differently at any point along the way, Josie may have felt greater comfort, rather than less, in seeking out her parents for their help and support.

AMY left home when she was eighteen and married her boyfriend, whom her entire family disliked. Her new husband wanted lots of children, so they had their first baby one year later. He started physically abusing her soon after the baby arrived. Five years later, Amy and her husband had three children and had lived in five different states. Her husband forbade her to call or write her family because "it was too expensive," so she hadn't spoken to them since the birth of their first child. That was just as well, in her mind, since her relatives made subtle disparaging comments about her husband.

Amy's parents and sisters knew only the address of the first apartment they had moved to and had sent her a few letters, but her husband had intercepted them all and torn them up without Amy's knowledge. When they didn't receive replies to their letters, her relatives felt angry and hurt, assuming that she wanted no part of them. When Amy failed to receive letters or calls from her relatives, she assumed that they had disowned her for marrying the man she chose. After the physical abuse began and the babies started to come, Amy grew more and more isolated and depressed.

Every time Amy made a friend, her husband somehow managed to lose his job and move them to a different state "seeking new opportunities." Once Amy struck up a friendship with another woman she met at the grocery store. As their friendship grew stronger Amy's husband began accusing her of having a secret affair during the time that she said she was with her new friend. He would go into jealous rages every time Amy planned to spend time with Vicki. Amy didn't want to risk losing Vicki's friendship by telling her the embarrassing truth directly, so she dropped hints to Vicki about her husband's abuse. She mentioned that her husband had a "jealous streak" and would "go ballistic" when she so much as looked at another man. Vicki thought this sounded normal and didn't ask more about it. Amy assumed that since Vicki thought her husband's behavior was normal, it must be acceptable. She tried to put the nagging feelings of sadness and anger out of her mind.

As her husband's abuse worsened, Amy began making up excuses for why she couldn't see Vicki, hoping that her husband would realize she wasn't having an affair and stop his jealous rages. Vicki eventually stopped calling her. When Vicki stopped calling, Amy assumed Vicki didn't like her anymore, so she didn't call Vicki either. They never spoke again.

As Amy grew more isolated, her husband became more violent. Amy became so depressed that she attempted to kill herself by cutting her wrists. It was during her hospitalization that she was finally able to tell a social worker of her husband's abuse. That was the first of many changes Amy would make in her life.

In Amy's experience, physical distance helped perpetuate the emotional distance from her family which had begun early in Amy's marriage to her abusive husband. It wasn't that Amy didn't love her family or that they didn't love her. It was a series of misunderstandings, orchestrated in part by Amy's husband, which put the finishing touches on the resentments which had started years before.

Amy's blossoming friendship with Vicki was marred by a series of assumptions made by each, assumptions about each other's reactions made without checking out how the other was actually feeling and why the other was acting the way she was. Ultimately both Amy and Vicki decided not to call each other again based on the culmination of these false assumptions.

Had Amy or any one of her relatives or Vicki taken action to remove themselves from the arms race, things might have progressed differently. Fortunately, Amy's silent cries for help, in the form of her suicide attempt, were heard and she was able to take advantage of the professional help provided, turning tragedy into hope.

JOHN was happily married with two children and a good job when he got a call from his sister, Phyllis, who lived in another state. She told him that her husband had beaten her up the night before. She was in a safe place today, but planned to leave her husband and the town they lived in as soon as possible. She asked John if she could move in with him and his family while she got her life in order. He said, "Of course," and helped make flight arrangements for the following day. The next day, Phyllis called John to say that she had changed her mind. Her husband was very sorry for treating her "badly" and she believed that he would never hurt her again, so she was going to stay with him.

Feeling very protective and extremely worried by her decision, John tried desperately to talk her into following through with her original plan to leave her husband. When that didn't work, he told her he would fly out to her house to "talk with her" more about her decision. Though it angered her that he didn't respect her decision, she passively said O.K. and agreed to pick him up at the airport. On the day of his arrival Phyllis was an hour late picking him up, claiming that she almost forgot that he was coming. Throughout the weekend of his stay John tried to get Phyllis alone so he could talk her into leaving her husband.

Phyllis and her husband carried on their lives in the blissful way they did immediately after a "blowup" and weren't anxious for Phyllis to spend private time with John. When it came time for John to leave, Phyllis took him to the airport. John was so angry and frustrated by that time, "for coming all the way out here for nothing!" that he told Phyllis if she didn't leave her husband now, she couldn't call him again for help later. To that Phyllis replied, "I didn't ask you to come here in the first place." They parted, both furious with the other. As she left the airport, Phyllis ambivalently crossed John off her mind's list, "That's one more person I can never go to for help."

In each of these stories the resentments that developed might have been avoided if just one of the involved parties had seen the destructive patterns and had risked pulling out of the race by reacting differently. The arms race can't be a race if there's only one participant.

YOUR PROCESS WILL BE UNIQUE

You may have feelings and beliefs other than the ones mentioned here because you are a unique individual, just as the woman you care about is unique. The important thing is to try to identify your own feelings and beliefs about domestic violence issues. Educate yourself with the facts before you alienate your battered friend or relative without realizing what you are doing. Everyone has biases. Become more aware of yours and try to keep an open mind. Your mind will open further as you hear and learn more.

CHAPTER THREE

———⊶⊷———

To Learn:
Fundamental Information

For most battered women I've known, information was the key to freedom. For you, information could be the key to an abused woman's mind and ultimately her heart: Is she being abused? If so, what does that mean for her life? What must she be experiencing, thinking, and feeling? Why does she act the way she does?

By contradicting untruths and correcting myths, information will effectively break down the reef which stands between you, helping you see and hear her better. As the reality of her situation comes into view you can determine if and how you can be of help. Once this is done, she will feel safer to set a course in your direction.

The knowledge is for your own enlightenment, not hers. Though it's very tempting to share with her what you are learning about domestic violence, wait to do that until you feel very comfortable in the role as anchor, when you are equipped to decide how, when, and what information you might offer.

SEEING HER WITH NEW EYES

A battered woman may not be an expert concerning her own situation. In fact, because she is trapped in an unpredictable relationship in which she experiences the high of true love one moment and the depths of sadness and hurt the next, a battered woman can be like a ship tossed helplessly about by the waves. She may have difficulty realizing her predicament because, in order to survive her circumstances, she doesn't listen to or trust her own instincts. For most of us, these instincts preserve us from harm. She may have, to some extent, ignored that inner voice which tells her what is safe and what is dangerous. She may not realize she needs help or support, and denies the danger of her position. Furthermore, she may not even comprehend that there are people out there who can furnish a sense of stability and acceptance. Therefore, you may need to make your own assessment about the seriousness of her situation. Below are some cues to help.

SIGNS OF ABUSE: POWER AND CONTROL

In order to determine if your friend or relative might be in a physically abusive relationship (and therefore might need your help), you can look at the way control is played out in her relationship and the way she behaves in response to it.

In a physically abusive relationship there is a significant

imbalance of control, with the batterer actively taking and maintaining much more control over his partner than she has over him. This does not mean that she doesn't attempt to control him in some ways. She probably does. The key thing to notice is who usually gets his or her needs met and at whose expense. In a physically abusive relationship the batterer's needs are served at the expense of the victim's needs.

If you see that your friend or relative is involved in a relationship with a significant imbalance of power, be aware that this relationship may be or have a potential to become physically abusive. For the purpose of this discussion, WHERE THERE IS A SIGNIFICANT IMBALANCE OF POWER IN A PRIMARY LOVE RELATIONSHIP, THERE MAY ALSO BE PHYSICAL ABUSE.

Few relationships will exhibit visible and obvious signs of abuse to most outsiders. That doesn't mean indicators aren't there. The batterer might be abusing carefully and "behind closed doors" so that outsiders won't notice the signs. For example, most batterers are careful to bruise their victims on parts of the body which will be covered by clothes. Many batterers save their belittling comments for private conversations. You will probably have to be fairly close to a couple to see signs of abuse. Several people I know have discovered that their friends or relatives were abused by their partners only after going on a vacation with the couple. It was too difficult for them to keep up their happy couple facade over the course of several days. In some cases, even people who are very close to a couple will not see any indications of abuse.

It is also important to keep in mind that the existence of one individual sign may not mean that there is abuse in the relationship. For example, a miscarriage or series of

---

miscarriages may or may not signal violence in a relationship; one must look at all other aspects of the situation before making that kind of assessment. So, I caution you to read the following signs of abuse carefully and with responsibility. If you do see some of the signs discussed in this chapter within a woman's relationship, respect her enough to check out any concerns you have directly with her before you jump to any false conclusions (see, in Chapter Five, "Asking Her Sensitive Questions").

In this section I have outlined three areas in which power in abusive relationships is commonly out of balance: emotional, physical, and circumstantial. Please note that these signs cannot be whittled down to a checklist. They involve complex dynamics which must be observed over time.

EMOTIONAL ABUSE

POTENTIAL BATTERERS ALMOST ALWAYS ABUSE THEIR PARTNERS ON AN EMOTIONAL LEVEL BEFORE THEY PHYSICALLY ABUSE THEM; the emotional abuse continues and often gets worse after the physical abuse has begun. By emotional abuse I mean that a batterer attempts to control what his partner believes, feels, or does through means of intimidation or manipulation.

How can you spot emotional abuse among couples you know? As friend or relative, you might see the batterer consistently putting his partner down; e.g., "My wife could sure stand to lose fifty pounds and learn how to cook." Or, more blatantly, "Honey, you're so ugly, you would never find another man if you left me." He may call her derogatory names or refer to her as such in front of you. However, just as often, batterers hold their partners high upon a pedestal; she can do no wrong, they were born to be to-gether, she's an angel sent to be only with him. He may show his adoration of her in ways her friends envy, regu-larly bringing gifts or flowers, taking her to nice restau-rants, etc. The tendency to worship their partners is common to batterers and is a clue in itself: it masks the obsessiveness, jealousy, and possessiveness which also characterizes bat-terers. When she does "fall from grace," she has a long way to fall.

A man's attempting to intimidate his partner with a cer-tain "look" when he doesn't think others are watching is another sign of emotional abuse. For example, she makes a comment he dislikes, and he responds by sending her a quick, punitive glance. The message he sends: "If you don't shut your mouth I'll hurt you." In response to his message she might immediately change her behavior so as to do his bidding. This private code or shorthand is unspoken, yet an important clue when you feel its power to create fear and submission: it can fill the room, and produce a light-ning response. You might notice that the couple's children respond similarly to the code.

There is a chronic use of intimidating signals and belit-tling comments in abusive relationships which puts the majority of the power in the relationship on the abuser's side. The existence of the code signifies an imbalance in the relationship. When one person has such power on an ongoing basis, one look can be deadening. There can be a feeling of uneasiness so strong between partners that even outsiders can feel it. You might feel it when you are with them.

If you are around a woman by herself more often than the couple, you might notice signs in her behavior of the emotional abuse she is experiencing. You might first observe that she isolates herself from people and activities she once cared about. She may be shying away from making new friends, be more reserved around old friends, or no longer go places she once frequented. She may quit her job or school or otherwise withdraw from the life that she lived before she met her partner. She may constantly seek permission from her partner before doing anything, or check with him often while she is away from him. In general, she may not feel free to choose what she does or does not do. She may begin to feel and speak badly about herself, her appearance, or her abilities. Many women who have lived within an abusive relationship for a while or after a particularly violent incident have trouble concentrating and seem to be in a fog. She might directly complain that her partner thinks she's not good enough or otherwise belittles her. She may tell you that he harasses her by driving by her job to check up on her or that he listens in on phone conversations. She may admit that he won't let her go certain places because he doesn't want her screwing around on him.

If you hear your friend or relative making self-demeaning comments, if she complains that her partner belittles her, or if her partner seems to control where she goes and what she does, file that information away in your brain, and listen to her all the more carefully.

PHYSICAL SIGNS OF ABUSE

The most obvious physical signs of abuse are bruises, cuts, red marks, internal injuries, broken bones, or injuries caused by objects, anywhere on her body, which seem to happen frequently or for which she doesn't have an explanation that rings true. MOST BATTERERS BEGIN THEIR

USE OF PHYSICAL ABUSE BY HURTING THEIR PART-
NERS IN WAYS WHICH DON'T LEAVE MARKS OR BY
LEAVING MARKS IN PLACES WHERE THEY CAN'T BE
SEEN BY OUTSIDERS. Therefore, if you witness a more
obvious physical sign of abuse on your loved one, it is
probably not the first.

Less obvious physical signs of abuse are such things as
broken household items (furniture, glass), holes in walls, or
torn clothing. When police respond to a domestic violence
call they view these as evidence of domestic abuse. If you
notice the existence of some of the other signs within a
loved one's relationship and there is always something
getting broken or torn at her house, that may be further in-
dication of violence within her relationship.

CIRCUMSTANTIAL SIGNS OF ABUSE

A BATTERER'S PATTERN IS TO ISOLATE HIS PART-
NER AND MAKE HER TOTALLY DEPENDENT UPON
HIM PSYCHOLOGICALLY AND FINANCIALLY, SO
SHE CAN'T EASILY LEAVE HIM WHEN HIS ABUSE
ESCALATES. Thus, you may begin to notice circumstantial signs of abuse, things happening to your friend or relative directly resulting from her relationship which seem
not to be in her best interest. Her life has significantly
changed, and the changes do not support her personal happiness or growth. For instance, she might once have been
content to live in one place for a while, near friends and
jobs or school. Now, since getting involved with her partner, she moves her residence frequently or makes a significant move away from her support systems (family, friends,
or job). Frequent moves are a common circumstantial sign
of abuse. They serve to keep an abused woman isolated,

without access to help should she want to leave the relationship.

Financial control is a common circumstantial sign of an abusive relationship. If he keeps control over the purse strings, her options are seriously limited. I've seen women who made $50,000+ a year at their own jobs whose batterers have arranged things so that they have access to none of it, and therefore no money for a hotel or transportation should they decide to leave. Perhaps the woman you care about never has spending money or she declines invitations to participate in activities she enjoys, saying her partner won't *allow* her to spend money on such things. Or, maybe she states directly that her partner controls the money. Some abused women readily accept this aspect of their partner's control, viewing him as the "head of the household," that he *should* control the money.

I recall one case in which the husband demanded that his wife hand over her paycheck to him each payday; he would promptly deposit it into an account with only his name on it (she had signed a signature card to have her name added to the account, but he had secretly disposed of it). He told both his wife and me that he deposited the money directly into this account for her own good because she wasn't responsible enough with spending. In actuality, he was gradually taking away her avenues of freedom at the same time that he was becoming more and more physically abusive. When she did leave him and went to the account to withdraw her half of their money for living expenses, the bank informed her that her name had never been added to the account, so she couldn't withdraw any money from it. Needless to say, it was terribly frustrating and embarrassing for this woman (a woman with a high-paying, stable career) to then have to come to our battered women's shelter asking for basic assistance.

ABOUT THE CHILDREN

Though many of the children who live in violent families appear to be quite normal, they are likely to be plagued by powerful and distracting emotions of anger, resentment, fear, and sadness. Some children seem to be especially responsible and competent, when actually this pseudo-mature behavior (acting more adultlike than one would expect of someone that age) masks low self-esteem and in-security. Other children are overly clingy with adults other than their parents. Still other children who live in violent families isolate themselves from social contact and many have difficulty controlling their own behavior.

Imagine yourself as a child who lives in a home where one parent abuses the other; waiting through the days, weeks, or months of the buildup of tension, the small incidents—father slamming his fist down on the table or holding mother in her chair so that she will sit and listen to yet another of his lectures. Then, one day, mother tells you to go to your room because she just got a call from dad that he's coming home early. He's mad and he needs to "talk" to her. Envision what it is like for that child to sit, huddled in the bedroom, listening—the slam of the car door, the slam of the back door, dad's booming voice, mom's pleas and explanations, thundering footsteps, crashes against the wall, breaking glass, screams of fear and pain, cursing, name-calling, ground-quaking thuds on the floor, sobbing, and on and on and on for a seemingly endless length of time.

If you have never been in fear for your life or the life of someone you depend on and love as deeply as your mother, it will probably be hard to put yourself in the place of that child. The child must tiptoe around quietly, just as his mother must do, never knowing when dad is going to blow up. The child must spend so much emotional energy surviving the waves of violence, there is not much energy left to daydream, develop a peaceful inner world, or practice trusting others.

Many children who live in homes where there is spouse abuse are also physically or sexually abused or neglected themselves by one or both parents (see Appendix V, "Child Abuse and Neglect," if you suspect that a child is being abused or neglected). Men who batter their partners also tend to abuse their children. A batterer's need and ability to control his partner through violence can easily extend to controlling his child. Even unborn children are at risk of being physically abused by their violent fathers. Batterers often become more violent toward their partners during pregnancies, at a time when the women are particularly dependent on them for financial and emotional subsistence; the ultimate form of control. I had a client whose husband raped her repeatedly until she became pregnant, then he beat her on the abdomen claiming that she got pregnant on purpose to spite him. Batterers do tend to beat their pregnant partners on and around the abdomen where the fetus is living and growing, which is especially dangerous for an unborn child. A woman who has been beaten during her pregnancy is much more likely to miscarry or deliver prematurely, which can result in long-term serious medical problems for the mother or infant.

Batterers do not always physically abuse their children or their pregnant partners. Many of my clients reported to me that their husband's abuse was quite focused on them and not directed toward the children. Some women said that their partner's abuse of them actually stopped during their pregnancies but resumed after the baby was born.

Many people have difficulty recognizing that some battered women are abusive parents. Some of these women overdiscipline at the demands of their partners ("You teach that kid a lesson or I'll teach you one"). Others are so stressed from living within the tension-filled house caused by their partner's abuse that they explode toward the only safe person, the child. Still other women never learned how to parent without using abusive tactics. Perhaps they were abused as children or saw their parents hurt each other, and they now carry on the abusive legacy.

Whether or not they are physically abused or neglected themselves, it is extremely emotionally damaging for children to live in a family where there is partner abuse. Indeed, THE EMOTIONAL DAMAGE CAUSED WHEN ONE PARENT HURTS THE OTHER OFTEN AFFECTS THE CHILD AS SIGNIFICANTLY AS IF THE ABUSE IS DIRECTED TOWARD THE CHILD. It makes no difference, from a child's perspective, whether dad is pointing his gun at mom or he's pointing the gun at him/herself. Either way is terrifying! This is not even to consider the lack of parental energy going into the child's development. Men who batter usually don't have the emotional maturity necessary to properly nurture their children. Women who are battered rarely have the emotional or physical energy left to sufficiently nurture their children. They're focusing on trying to survive.

Many battered women I have worked with believed that they owed it to their kids to have a father around, especially if he was good to the children. They believed that to leave their husband would be to deny their child a basic right, having a father-figure. They had read or heard how devastating divorce is and didn't want their children to suffer that way. Until they sought counseling, many of my clients didn't see how their being abused by their partners even affected their children. Since they were careful to hide bruises and not let their kids directly witness abusive episodes, they believed the children didn't know about the abuse. Despite their mother's valiant attempts to conceal the violence at home, in counseling the children would usually express a painful awareness of it, even if they didn't know what to call it.

The effects on children of growing up in a violent family are not only visible in many cases to the anchor but serious and significant for all of us. Several studies have indicated that men who grew up in violent families are much more likely to become abusive partners than men from nonviolent families.[1] Children learn from their parents; if they have a parent who uses violence to handle problems within intimate relationships, the children learn that violence is an acceptable way to behave in those relationships. Acceptance of violence is passed down from generation to generation in this way. THIS GENERATION'S CHILDREN FROM VIOLENT FAMILIES ARE THE NEXT GENERATION'S BATTERERS AND VICTIMS.

It will be reassuring to a potential anchor that not only can the children lend clues about battering, but being an anchor for a battered woman will indirectly benefit her child. An anchor can support a battered woman in her burgeoning self-awareness so that she can gain the confidence needed to make the best decisions for herself and her

[1] Richard J. Gelles and Claire Pedrick Cornell, *Intimate Violence in Families* (Newbury Park, Calif.: Sage Publications, 1990), p. 76.

children. An anchor can also sometimes help make it financially and practically possible for the battered woman to choose to leave an abusive partner so that her children can live without violence. An anchor's caring ear may help a battered woman come to the recognition that her child is being negatively affected by the violence. This realization may, in turn, be a powerful motivator for her. In my counseling practice it was when a mother saw her child(ren) being hurt physically or emotionally by the violence that a siren would go off in her head blaring, *THE VIOLENCE MUST STOP!* For the sake of their children, many of my clients did, indeed, find ways to leave their batterers, and some were able to encourage their partners into therapy designed to help them stop abusing others. An anchor can provide a safe tie where there was only fear and helplessness before, giving a battered woman hope where she had none; hope that she can hand down to her children.

ANOTHER SIGN: "THE CYCLE OF VIOLENCE"[2]

If you have had the opportunity to be the confidante of a battered woman or to observe a possibly abusive relationship for some time, you may find the relationship goes through predictable phases, described as the "cycle of violence" by Lenore Walker in her book *The Battered Woman*. Walker's chapter on the "cycle of violence" was one of the single most helpful resources I had in my work with battered women. It had such impact that I would discuss the cycle with all new clients who were being battered by their partners. The response of most of those women was, "Oh

[2] Lenore E. Walker, *The Battered Woman* (New York: Harper & Row, 1971), pp. 55–70.

my gosh, that describes my relationship!" Furthermore, their ways of thinking about their relationships and partners were often significantly altered from that point on. When Jackie first starting reading about battered women, she found Walker's cycle to be the most enlightening piece of information of any she had read.

THE STAGES IN "THE CYCLE OF VIOLENCE"

1. Tension-Building Stage—"Minor" abusive incidents occur (e.g., he throws objects, hits walls, cusses, belittles, yells). He blames someone or something else for causing his upset. She may deny her angry feelings and rationalize away his behavior as she anxiously looks for ways to smooth the way for him, so he won't move into the next, more severely violent, stage. Her efforts to control his violence may seem to work for a while but are invariably futile as the tension becomes too great and they move into the next stage. Indeed, some women unconsciously push their partners toward the next stage so that they can relieve the tension between them and feel some control within their relationship, however short-lived.

2. Acute Battering Incident—Characterized by his extreme, unpredictable, out-of-control violence, the actual type of beating can take on an infinite number of forms. She knows she has no control over what he does to her or when he will stop. She senses that he will hurt her worse should she resist or fight back in any way, and she knows it will do no good to try to escape. She is completely terrified, often paralyzed with fear. Her survival mechanism kicks in and she might dissociate herself from the beating, psychologically removing her mind from her body so as

not to feel the physical pain of the beating. The incident can last for a few minutes or several days.

When the violence is over, she may initially react with shock or disbelief. As a result, she might not seek help for several days after the incident, if she seeks help at all. After a few days she may begin to feel sadness, anger, and helplessness. It is at the end of this stage and the beginning of the next that she is most likely to leave the relationship.

3. Kindness and Contrite Loving Behavior—The calm after the storm or, as battered women I've known prefer, "honeymoon" phase. He is apologetic for the beating and tries to justify his behavior. He promises to never do it again and believes that he won't. He tells her how much he needs her, perhaps even threatening to commit suicide if she does not come back to him. He may be so convincing and she may want so desperately for the relationship to feel the way it once did that she accepts his apology and believes his promises, or even his justification. The relationship feels blissful again, as it did in the beginning. They feel the chemistry we are all taught to expect of true love. What occurs during this stage bonds them together like glue.

The cycle repeats itself again and again, usually becoming more frequent and more severe over time. IN AN ONGOING RELATIONSHIP THERE IS VIRTUALLY NO SUCH THING AS ONE VIOLENT INCIDENT.

EMOTIONAL IMPACT ON A BATTERED WOMAN OF LIVING IN THE CYCLE

You may observe that living within the cycle means a lot of emotional ups and downs. It is very difficult to push your own feelings and needs aside on a daily basis in hopes that your partner won't blow up. When it doesn't work and your partner does become violent, your world comes crashing down around you as heavily as if it were the first abusive incident. Then, things are immediately better and the cycle begins again. To live with these highs and lows over months and years is extremely disorienting and takes its toll on a person's psyche. But despite how traumatized the victim of abuse is, the nature of the cycle of violence is such that it invites her to stay in it.

As the relationship progresses and the violence cycles again and again, the roles each person assumes change. Classic characteristics of the batterer and victim begin to emerge and may be visible to outsiders. He shows his possessiveness and extreme jealousy while she becomes more appeasing. He blames her and other people for his misbehavior or faults. She may either begin to accept that blame or resent him for not accepting responsibility for his violence. He shows his tendency toward dominance and control while she grows more passive and hurt, or perhaps angry and passive-aggressive. He begins to behave more irrationally and unpredictably. She responds with confusion, general anxiety, depression, and feelings of helplessness.

A woman who is in an abusive relationship usually experiences great inner turmoil. Over time, her thoughts run the gamut. At one point she might think, "O.K., he beat me again, but this time he means it when he promises to go to counseling and get real help. He loves me. He won't do it again." At another point she might express, "Things are going so great for us. This new job of his is just what is going to change things," or, "Little things are starting to make him mad again. The kids and I are walking on eggshells, just waiting for him to blow up. I hope it doesn't happen right before I have to be at work next time." At yet another time she might feel, "That jerk, he really hurt me bad this time. I thought he was going to kill me. I'm leaving for good. He's never going to change."

Such diverse thoughts and feelings show how conflicted she must be on the inside, not even considering what she deals with on the outside; helping children with their feelings, trying to smooth out her partner's life in a vain attempt to control his violence, plus the everyday life pressures we all face. She probably does a good job of hiding these feelings and pressures, so don't be surprised if she looks like a confident, calm, assertive, happy person. Indeed, she probably feels that way at times. It is important for you to know, however, that while she is living with her batterer another side of her is probably experiencing a roller coaster of feelings and thoughts.

You may find, as a potential anchor, that those very characteristics that distance you from her are signs of the seriousness of your abused friend's or relative's situation and her need for an anchor. Living in the chaos of the cycle of violence tends to alienate the victim of abuse from those very people who care about her and might be able to help. Relatives and friends of battered women often grow exasperated with the turmoil—one minute she leaves him and says she's gone for good. The next minute she's back with him and claims everlasting love. Staying closely connected to her becomes very painful. So in helplessness and despair they often give up their connections with her.

ANSWERS TO COMMONLY ASKED QUESTIONS

Who are Battered Women?

BATTERED WOMEN COME FROM ALL BACKGROUNDS. She can be rich or poor, of any color or ethnicity. She can be a lawyer or married to a police officer. She can be politically liberal or conservative. She can go to church every Sunday or never have set foot in one. She can be psychologically normal (at least before the battering began) or she can be emotionally ill. She can be any woman. She is me.

I am from an upper-middle-class, stable, nonviolent family. My father was a college professor and my mother was a college-educated, full-time homemaker. I met Joe just before graduating from college (as a social worker specializing in psychotherapy, no less) and dated him for three years. Through the years he had "tested" me several times (see Chapter Seven for more about testing). I knew he had a bad temper and was somewhat irresponsible, but I didn't admit to myself that he might be dangerous to me until I tried to break up with him. He hit me once, then apologized and begged my forgiveness. Until that time I had always believed that people behaved logically and that it wouldn't be logical for him to risk hurting me again, so I agreed to see him once more. It was during that last visit that he beat and terrorized me over the course of eight hours, threatening me with a gun and holding me against my will.

I still believe I might be dead today had I not escaped. What's unbelievable, especially to me, is that I was a practicing psychotherapist at the time this was happening. I was supposed to understand people and their behavior. Indeed, it took me several years of working with battered women to even identify myself as a battered woman. I, too, was embarrassed. I kept thinking that I was the exception, too smart to let that happen to me! I discovered that many battered women, before they meet other battered women, feel they are the exceptions. It could be argued that we are all exceptions since we are all unique, but such an argument isolates a woman from those who share with her the experience of being abused by a partner.

Why does she stay, or why does she keep returning to him?

Each woman has her own individual and complex reasons why she stays or returns to her batterer. Give your friend or relative the respect to try and understand *her* unique reasons. It takes energy away from your efforts toward becoming her anchor for you to spend much time speculating on probabilities or possibilities regarding her abuse experience. Listen to and be with her. That is what will help her.

To give you an idea of why some women choose to stay with or return to their abusive partners, I've listed common reasons here:

1. She loves the part of her partner that is not abusive.

2. She believes and hopes it will get better. By studying the cycle of violence you will see how her hopes are kept alive.

3. It is exciting and passionate. It feels good most of the time.

4. Because she doesn't know if or how she can get out or stay out safely.

5. She believes that being committed to someone means you stay through good and bad.

6. Her pride won't allow her a failed marriage (or *another* failed marriage).

7. She believes that her children need their father.

8. No one has ever loved her so much as her partner.

9. She can't financially support herself and her children without his income.

10. Staying is more comfortable than the unknown (of being alone).

11. She feels sorry for him since he has no one to love him besides her. She worries that her partner might fall apart should she leave him.

12. She has experienced so little control over her life within the abusive relationship that she now feels powerless to change it.

What are some of the reasons women leave their batterers for good?

What causes one woman to stay with her batterer and another to leave is, at the very least, complicated. Once she's involved, it is very dangerous, and perhaps fatal, to leave. Divorced or separated women reported being victimized by intimates more often (16 per 1,000 persons) than women who never married (7 per 1,000) or married women (1.5 per 1,000).[3] The year I worked in a shelter for battered women, in a major metropolitan area, out of nineteen women who had been killed by their batterers, all nineteen had been killed *after* leaving their relationship. It is dangerous to leave a batterer. It is dangerous to stay with a batterer.

Of course, many women are successful in leaving their batterers. One Texas study found that 63 percent of women abused during their lifetime had divorced or permanently left their abusive husband (or live-in partner).[4] People often forget that many women leave abusive partners after the first, second, or third time he uses violence against them. These women don't often seek any form of professional assistance, or even tell anyone of their experience, so we don't often hear about them.

Some of the reasons women leave:

1. Her abusive partner did something which was the last straw for her. It might have been a seemingly trivial thing, compared to the major abusive incidents. Nevertheless,

[3] U.S. Department of Justice, Bureau of Justice Statistics, Selected Findings, "Violence between Intimates," November 1994, NCJ-149259.

[4] Raymond H. C. Teske Jr., Ph.D., and Mary L. Parker, M.A., *Spouse Abuse in Texas: A Study of Women's Attitudes and Experiences* (Texas Department of Human Resources, 1983), p. 3.

something clicks inside her, causing her not to care for him or be willing to take it anymore.

2. She began making enough money to support herself (and her children, if she has them) without his income.

3. Her batterer started hurting their children or she began to see how damaging it was for the children to be exposed to the abuse perpetrated against her.

4. An anchor became available to her, helping her to feel supported and confident in her decision to leave and giving her an emotional connection to someone besides her abusive partner. A battered women's shelter is a good example of an anchor as it provides women with safety and support. Of course, an anchor can be anyone, maybe you.

I'm confused about the children. You are saying that living in a home where there is spouse abuse is emotionally damaging to the children and that I should report suspected child abuse to the proper authorities. If I know that my friend is being abused by her husband, should I report to child protective services that her children are being emotionally abused?

Unfortunately, state laws and courts in our country don't usually view a child living in a home where there exists spouse or partner abuse as being emotionally abused or neglected by virtue of that fact alone. This may change as judges and legislators are educated in the dynamics of domestic violence. You can certainly speak to your friend about your concern for the emotional and physical safety of her children. Hopefully, with you as her anchor, she can begin to see the effects on her children of living within a violent home.

If you feel strongly about this issue, you can advocate for changes in the law. You also have every right to make a report of child abuse or neglect which you deem appropriate, regardless of what the law says currently. The child protective services caseworker might tell you that they can't open a case based on spouse abuse alone, but you can still make a report. Changes happen when people refuse to accept the status quo.

Was it something I did or did not do which caused her to get into an abusive relationship?

Many family members and friends feel guilty that they somehow caused their loved ones to get into an abusive relationship. There are so many women who have been battered, and they are from lots of different backgrounds and positions in society, it doesn't make sense to solely blame a woman's upbringing for her current relationship circumstances.

I also look at it this way: there are so many potential batterers in our world, any woman is statistically likely to date a batterer at some point in her dating career. If you doubt this, just ask women you know, who will be honest with you, if they have ever dated someone who turned out to have a bad temper and showed signs of extreme jealousy or possessiveness. Those are early signs of a potential batterer, and many women have dated someone who exhibits those characteristics at some point, although they probably didn't label the guy as a batterer. Many women simply never date a guy long enough or become involved enough to become his victim. Since batterers start their abuse very subtly, and become violent only after a woman is emotionally (and often financially) tied to them, any woman can find herself involved with someone who turns out to be abusive.

A note to parents of battered women: I do appreciate the courage it takes parents to look at how they raised their daughter and what they might have done to contribute to her choosing or, more significant to my mind, staying with an abusive partner. If this explorative process helps you unite with your daughter, great! It can be so connecting to say to your daughter, "There are things we did as parents which we thought were right at the time but may have contributed to your current feelings of shame or despair or lack of confidence. Let's take a look at our relationship together." But if looking into the past would somehow cause greater distance between you, perhaps you can look at those issues yourself or with help from a qualified therapist before you attempt to explore them with her.

If domestic violence is so common, why don't I hear about it happening more in my friends' families?

You may believe that you, as a family member or friend of a battered woman, are in a rare situation to which others can't relate. The more you feel that way, and the more you refrain from discussing the issue, the more isolated you become. Relatives and friends of battered women often grow to feel very frustrated and lonely. You may not be aware of them yet but, THERE ARE PEOPLE WITH WHOM YOU ARE ACQUAINTED WHO KNOW AND CARE ABOUT A BATTERED WOMAN, JUST LIKE YOU. And, they probably have feelings similar to yours. If you embark on the process of becoming an anchor for the battered woman you care about, you will open yourself up so that you are likely to see and hear other family members and friends of battered women with whom you can share your experience.

When Jackie started talking to me about her sister's abusive marriage, she was certain that spouse abuse was a rare occurrence. She believed that she didn't know anyone who had been battered in a relationship other than her sister. Of course, she did know battered women, but wasn't aware of them because they hadn't disclosed their secrets to her. They hadn't done so because she had presented herself as someone who didn't want to hear uncomfortable personal information. Once she began listening effectively, asking open-ended questions, and sharing her own feelings with other people, they reciprocated and began telling her their stories. Over time, more and more of her friends and relatives disclosed to her that they had been abused. "They're coming out of the woodwork," Jackie once exclaimed. "Abuse really is a bigger problem than I thought."

Which group has more difficulty becoming anchors, friends or family members?

Friends of battered women often have different struggles in becoming anchors than do relatives of battered women. Friends don't have the history, role complexity, and emotional intensity (or "unfinished business") with their battered loved ones that relatives often do. For this reason friends often find it easier than relatives to bridge the distance which might exist between them and a battered friend. However, that same lack of history and emotional ties also makes it easier for a friend to discontinue the relationship with an abused friend at the first sign of difficulties, while a family member will always remain in the same family and is therefore compelled to pursue solutions to relationship strain.

What this means to you if you choose to do anchor work: give anchor work extra time and chances if you are a friend of an abused woman. You will be personally rewarded in the end. If you are a relative of an abused woman, the going can get really rough. Pace yourself by allowing yourself regular, time-limited breaks from the storm (as Jackie did by planning relaxing outings with friends) so you don't get overwhelmed. Try to recognize when you need a break so that you don't end up emotionally distancing too much during those rough times, because that will only make the anchor work more difficult over the long run. You will also be personally rewarded for your efforts, and optimally your family system and everyone in it will benefit.

As a family therapist I've seen remarkable transformations of members within a family and the family system itself, when even *one* family member puts forth the effort necessary to making positive changes happen. All families, no matter how broken they may be, have strengths. If you are the one person in your family doing the anchor work, try to identify and utilize your family's strengths to aid you in providing a supportive and caring environment on which the battered woman in your midst can rely. For instance, your family may have a lot of fun together or share a strong sense of loyalty to family members. Utilizing the strengths your family has to offer will give the abused woman in your midst a tremendous source of strength to tap into when she feels powerless.

The previous chapters were designed to help you assess more confidently the reality of your friend or relative's situation: Is her relationship abusive? How dangerous is it? Is there distance and isolation between you and her that needs to be bridged? How has this distance come about? Do you want to bridge the distance so you can be of help? These assessments are not easy and you will have accomplished a great deal when you reach this crossroad.

CHAPTER FOUR

―――∞∞∞―――

To Be Distancer,
Rescuer, or Anchor

Now that you believe your friend or relative is in an abusive relationship and you have a sense of how close your relationship is with her, it's time to focus on the part you play. If you really want to help her, how can you be the most effective?

THREE ROLES

Two roles which relatives and friends typically find themselves playing in their relationships with their abused loved one are distancer and rescuer. On the relationship spectrum you will find a distancer at one extreme and a rescuer at the other. In the middle is the anchor. As you read this chapter, you will be able to determine where you are currently in this spectrum, and where you might move in order to be a more effective helper.

ABUSED WOMAN

DISTANCER·············|···············|··········· ANCHOR ···········|················|················RESCUER

Distancers tend to remove themselves emotionally from their abused loved ones. Rescuers tend to become too involved in relationships. Anchors, on the other hand, strive to maintain an objective distance from those they care about, while remaining involved with them in a respectful, supportive way.

This book is designed to help you move toward the middle anchor role. As the diagram illustrates, by moving toward the middle, you are moving closer to your loved one. Despite the fact that they are on opposite sides of the spectrum, the distancer and rescuer have similar roles in that they create emotional distance between themselves and the woman they care about. In contrast, anchor is a connecting role.

If you can see where you are on this spectrum, you will have a good idea what you face in your work toward becoming an anchor. The further to one side you are, the more work you have ahead of you.

TO BE A DISTANCER

DAN, THE STRONGMAN

DAN was one father who wasn't going to let his daughter's abusive marriage tear his family apart. He was a take-charge kind of man who had lived his life and built a successful business with a "just do it" attitude. He didn't believe in "wallowing in self-pity" and "crying over spilt milk." When you face adversity you "pull yourself up by your bootstraps" and move on.

Dan loved his daughter, Cheryl, very much. When she left her husband after yet another violent incident and brought their three children to live with her parents, Dan was secretly hopeful and relieved: maybe this time she had left him for good. To her, however, he showed his optimism with a gruff, "I see you left him again." Dan couldn't bring himself to talk to Cheryl about her marriage, her ordeal, or the many complicated decisions facing her; after all, he might become emotional and that was a very uncomfortable state for Dan.

Cheryl desperately needed her father's support and acceptance. She wanted to approach him about her needs but was too afraid of his gruff response, which to her felt like rejection. Father and daughter carried on in virtual silence about anything that really mattered. Cheryl felt more and more alone and spoke with her husband on the phone more and more often.

Cheryl decided to give her marriage another try. When she told her parents that she was returning to her husband, her father panicked. He wasn't accustomed to feeling such profound sadness and fear, so it all came out as anger at Cheryl. He stormed around the house threatening this and that, but to no avail. He wasn't succeeding in changing her mind. Indeed, she responded to his threats with her own anger and ended the "discussion" by storming out of the house vowing never to return.

Dan was an extreme distancer who had been distant in relationships all his adult life. When his daughter came to him in crisis he reacted in his usual fashion, with emotional unavailability. As his daughter reacted to his distance with her own, Dan felt more and more out of control of the situation, and helpless to alter the course the relationship was taking. His frustration and fear finally erupted in the only outlet he knew, an angry explosion, which caused such damage to their relationship that it was very difficult to repair. Indeed, he had to work for months to regain Cheryl's trust, to prove to her that he would express his feelings rationally and without threat.

Barb, the Pacifist

BARB was the type of person who prided herself in her openness with people. She had lots of friends and believed herself to have a close family. When her friend Natalie began to drop hints about her husband's alcohol abuse, Barb asked her more about it. Natalie was rather evasive and quickly changed the subject. This happened each time Barb asked Natalie questions about her husband or her marriage. Natalie would make a joke or otherwise minimize as exaggerations her revelations to Barb about her husband's behavior, behavior which Barb had a nagging feeling might be abusive.

Natalie's evasiveness began to bother Barb, but she didn't know how to talk to her about it. Barb began to assume that maybe she was reading too much into Natalie's stories and she stopped asking her to elaborate on them. As Barb pulled away, Natalie increased the hints she was giving. Barb was confused by this, so she began not responding to Natalie's hints at all. Barb worked to keep her conversations with Natalie on lighter subjects. Natalie stopped dropping hints and on that level their friendship remained.

Barb, being a relatively mild distancer, was not always distant with others. Indeed, she attempted to connect with Natalie, but when her attempts to connect were met with

Natalie's resistance, she readily gave up. Barb presumed that Natalie did not want or need to be closer with her, when really the opposite was the case. Natalie desperately needed to confide in Barb, but was afraid of running her off if she asked directly for help, so she would drop hints and then hide behind her jokes and minimizations. Barb simply misinterpreted what Natalie was doing and backed off. Natalie, in turn, misinterpreted Barb's retreat to mean Barb didn't care about connecting further, and backed off herself. The stagnation in their relationship was not an outcome desired by either person; it was, in effect, caused by a misunderstanding.

DISTANCING DOESN'T WORK

As you can see from Dan's and Barb's stories, despite their loving intentions distancing worked only to separate them from their abused loved ones. Distancing will interfere with your ability to be helpful to your loved one, for chances are she is doing her own distancing, or her abusive partner is doing it for her. Should she become ready to seek help, if you are emotionally distant from her she will probably not choose you to confide in, or accept your offer of assistance.

For distancers who may be considering a change, the payoff for moving toward the middle is clear. You will become closer to people you care about, helpful without wearing your heart on your sleeve. You will have someone to depend on when *you* need help or just someone to listen. It can be done. Jackie is a good example of a moderate distancer who did it.

Jackie's Challenge

When Jackie was able to see what her sister was really experiencing in her abusive marriage, she was motivated to help. At one point before taking on anchor work, Jackie suddenly realized, "Here is *my* sister, living in extreme danger! How could I live with any other decision than to help her? She's my sister." But for Jackie to help Diane she first had to connect emotionally with her. To do that, she would have to change some aspects of her own personality, those aspects which held her distant from Diane as well as other people. She knew overcoming those tendencies would not be easy.

Here are some of her thoughts in her own words:

I really wanted to be the kind of person who had compassion for other people. I admired people who seemed to be able to care for others so readily, but I couldn't seem to do it myself. I didn't know how to begin. The task of learning to be a connected, caring person seemed so huge and unreachable. I had always been emotionally distant from others. I was too strong and driven for my own good. When one lacks compassion for oneself, there usually is not compassion for anyone else. A guarded distance masked by a joking, fun-loving nature kept me from getting bogged down in other people's problems. I was very attached to the characteristics I had and I didn't want to give them up: my confidence, energy, focus, assertiveness, take-charge attitude. I was under the impression that I would have to give up all the qualities I liked about myself if I were going to change enough to be an anchor. Indeed, at first I thought that I would need to be Diane's rescuer, as were other members of my family, in order to be helpful to her. But rescuers seemed to me to be so overly emotional and over-involved. I knew I didn't want to be like that.

What I have come to understand is that I didn't have to choose between being a rescuer or being a distancer. There was a middle ground: being an anchor. I could practice doing things like an anchor does them, trying on anchor characteristics a bit at a time to see how they fit. I didn't need to change my whole personality, just make minor additions and adjustments to the strengths I already have!

Jackie's moral obligation to her sister's welfare had pushed her past her hesitations to do the work toward becoming an anchor. She decided to try a few of the suggestions I made. Each time she tried on a new behavior she was surprised by how quickly and how well it worked. For example, she was amazed by the responses she got from her and her sister's mutual friends when she would ask, "How do you feel about that?" That simple question deepened conversations and therefore relationships much more readily than Jackie had imagined possible. Since her new way of acting was continually reinforced by the positive reactions of Diane and others, Jackie continued.

HOW TO KNOW IF YOU'RE A DISTANCER

If you find that you have difficulties making significant connections with people in your life, including the abused woman you care about, you may tend to be a distancer. Perhaps you rationalize away the distant nature of your relationships, "I don't need to depend on anyone but myself. Close relationships can be so complicated and hard. Who needs them?" Perhaps, on the other hand, you wish you had closer relationships like other people seem to have, but you just don't know how to achieve them.

If you tend to be a distancer, learning anchor tools (the subject of Chapters Five and Six) can help you open yourself up to deeper relationships while remaining reasonably protected from emotional or physical harm. Granted, you may have to risk some rejection to be an anchor with an abused woman you care about. She may not trust your intentions or be able to reciprocate your overtures right away. But the potential rewards are much greater than the risk. As you saw in Dan's and Barb's stories, distancing causes its own pain. You may need to decide which risk is greater, the risks associated with getting closer to someone or the risks associated with remaining distant.

TO BE A RESCUER

ERIN, THE CAREGIVER

ERIN was always there when any of her friends needed her, so much so that they had nicknamed her "mother." When Erin's roommate, Julie, mentioned to her that her boyfriend, Jack, was verbally abusive, Erin said she could talk to her about it night or day. She gave Julie lots of "helpful" advice and followed through with reminders and encouragement. Erin read all the books she could find on verbally abusive relationships and then gave them to Julie to read. She would discuss the important points in the book and relate them to Julie's relationship.

Erin, too, had experienced abuse in a dating relationship and felt that she knew exactly what Julie was feeling. But when Erin was around Jack and Julie, she didn't quite know how to behave. It was as if Erin knew a secret about Jack that she wasn't supposed to know, so she pretended to the couple to know nothing of the abuse. Yet Erin couldn't help hating Jack for what he was doing to her friend.

As Erin's frustration increased she found herself "forgetting" to give Julie the message that Jack called. Once, when he was over to their apartment for dinner, Jack referred to Julie as a bitch. That was the last straw. Erin's anger rushed to the surface, and before she knew it she had cussed at him and ordered him never to set foot on their property again. The next day Julie moved out of their apartment and in with Jack. Erin and Julie never saw each other again.

Erin was an extreme rescuer, regularly taking action to help her friends without their direction or even permission. She believed that a good friend was proactive, always available to help a friend in need. That's how she showed she cared.

In her zealous way of helping, however, Erin became overly involved in her friends' lives and took too personally the things which happened or decisions they made. She also drew a lot of conclusions about what they needed and how they felt based on her own feelings and experiences. Meanwhile her friends began to resent Erin's help as they felt more and more controlled by her. At the same time, Erin couldn't understand why her help was not embraced. She had such good intentions, it seemed to her. As the friend would back away, Erin would tighten her grip of control (in the form of more help). To Erin's surprise, the friendship would often end in some kind of blowup or disagreement.

JIM, THE PROTECTOR

JIM saw himself as a reasonable, caring guy. When he found out from his parents that his sister, Ashley, had been beaten up by her boyfriend, he was shocked but able to maintain his composure.

When he spoke with his sister she minimized the whole experience; her boyfriend was under a lot of pressure in his job, he would never mean to hurt her, she had started the argument which led to the beating, he never hit her with his fist so it wasn't really abuse, etc. Jim listened attentively but without comment, appalled at his sister's ability to rationalize away her boyfriend's violence. He tried to stay busy and not think too much about his sister's relationship.

One day Ashley called to say that her boyfriend had hurt her again and she needed help. That was all Jim needed. Without asking what kind of help she wanted, Jim got off the phone and immediately began making preparations for her safety. He arranged for her to stay with a family friend, called the battered women's shelter to ask about counseling services for her, and called the district attorney's office to ask how to obtain a protective order. When Ashley arrived at his house she made it clear that she didn't like any of the plans he had made for her. She wasn't sure what she wanted to do next. Jim spent the next few hours trying to talk Ashley into doing what he had planned. She sat, zoned out, while he droned on and on. When he was done, Ashley got up and left to go stay with another family member.

Jim was a moderate rescuer. Only selected people pushed his rescuer buttons; when a person he cared about and felt protective of was in trouble (especially his little sister!) he felt compelled to do whatever needed to be done. When his sister resisted his attempts to help, he just became more frantic and tried every way he knew to talk her into doing what he thought was best. Ultimately, he couldn't make her see things his way. Indeed, she felt less empowered the more he talked, so she left to stay with someone who could support *her* decisions.

RESCUING DOESN'T WORK

There are times when to act on a woman's behalf without her direction is indicated (see Chapter Six for that discussion), but generally, rescuing a battered woman doesn't help her.

As you can see, Erin's and Jim's ways of helping their loved ones did not actually help them. Instead, their rescue attempts resulted in greater distance between them. Indeed, rescuing often results in the opposite of what was intended: although most rescuers I've known believe they are close to their abused loved ones, the opposite may actually be the case. Remember, a close emotional connection requires mutual trust and respect. You may care very deeply for an abused woman. You may want desperately to see that she doesn't get hurt or killed by her abusive partner. As hard as this may be to understand, by attempting to rescue her you are not *showing* your support of her. You are not *showing* her that you respect her or her abilities to make decisions and take action to protect herself. Or, as the case may be, you are not empowering her to improve upon those abilities. *You are not helping her.* If you are rescuing her, you may actually be removing your support and disempowering her.

To rescue a woman from her abusive partner or her life as it exists can even be an implied criticism of her. You are sending her a message that she could easily interpret as, "You are a screw-up. You make bad decisions which have gotten you into this horrible mess. Since you are a bad decision maker and since I make better decisions than you, you should do what I am telling you, not what you are telling yourself!" I know that might sound pretty severe and probably not what you would mean in your attempts to save your loved one from an abusive relationship. You are just concerned about her safety. Nevertheless, the effect on an abused woman, who is already demoralized from the abuse, is usually that she feels further criticized and discounted, treated like a child.

Your rescue attempts may be more a function of your own needs rather than what is best for her. Perhaps it is natural to try to grab control of a situation you feel particularly powerless over and frightened about, which are feelings family members and friends often have. But it is important that you look at your own agenda in rescuing her. Will it help her feel more confident, capable? Or is it actually designed to make you feel better, more in control of your own uncomfortable feelings? If the latter better describes your situation, it will be more productive for you to focus on your own feelings and needs rather than hers.

Rescuing is a form of overcontrol which demoralizes, and in a sense further abuses, the recipient. Most adults have an intrinsic need to feel capable of making their own decisions and doing what is necessary to make those decisions a reality. Women who are in abusive relationships have those same needs. If an abused woman you know perceives your rescue attempts as overcontrol, she is likely to distance herself emotionally from you in order to regain a sense of self-control and mature independence.

Moreover, rescuing an abused woman may actually support her abusive partner's control over her. When a battered woman has been told time and again, by the man who is supposed to love her, that she is weak, or a poor decision maker, or lazy, or ugly or fat or dumb, she may begin to believe it. When relatives or friends who are supposed to love her also make decisions for her or otherwise control her life, she will be even more likely to believe her partner's negative descriptions of her. She might conclude, "How can my husband, friends, and family all be wrong about me? None of them believe I can do anything right on my own."

In some instances I encountered, the battered woman *wanted* to be rescued because she didn't feel capable of making her own tough decisions. The problem was, in almost every case I can recall in which the woman was rescued by someone, she ended up returning, and rather quickly at that, to her abusive partner. Of course, battered women usually do return to their partners several times before their final break, but the women I knew usually returned more quickly when they were rescued. And the more quickly a woman returns, the less likely she is to have had enough time to grow emotionally from the separation experience. So, as tempting as it might be to rescue a battered woman, it won't work to keep her safe in the long run.

HOW TO KNOW IF YOU'RE A RESCUER

You may have rescuer tendencies if you tend to assume a director role in loved ones' lives when you see the need. You may view yourself as the kind of person who will do anything to help someone you care about. You are there at a moment's notice to make quick decisions and get things done, even as others seem to be faltering. It seems so clear what needs to be done. Perhaps you are a natural leader, efficient and organized. Perhaps it is excruciatingly painful to stand by and do nothing as someone you care about suffers. Yet as hard as you work, loved ones never seem to fully appreciate your well-intentioned help.

By rescue I mean that you are taking action *on her behalf* which is controlled and directed by you, not by her. Control is the operative word here. To control someone else with the best of intentions is not far removed from controlling someone with less pure intentions. Indeed, many abusive men think of themselves as having good intentions, while they control their partners. I can't tell you how many batterers I've worked with who justified their abuse and control of their partners with, "She wouldn't do what I wanted her to do, so I *had* to . . . to teach her a lesson."

There are many ways to rescue a battered woman. A friend of one of my clients simply walked into my client's apartment, packed her things, and took her to live in her home, even though my client kept quietly protesting that she didn't want to move out. That very night, after her friend went to sleep, my client called her husband; he picked her up and moved her still-packed things back to their apartment. Her friend felt betrayed and angry at what she viewed as my client's wishy-washy behavior. The parents of another one of my clients attempted to rescue their daughter from her abusive relationship by offering her money to return to college, contingent upon her leaving her batterer. She didn't leave him and never returned to college. They felt totally frustrated, their hands tied.

Suffice it to say, if the woman you care about did not think of a plan herself, be wary of your own need to take over the decision making for her. If you choose to be her rescuer, your focus will be on changing her. If you choose to be her anchor, your focus will be on getting yourself into a position to help.

KATE'S RESCUE ATTEMPT

Earlier in this chapter I told you about Jackie's tendency to distance from her abused sister Diane. Now I'd like to introduce you to Kate, who is Jackie and Diane's middle sister. Since childhood, Kate and Diane have been best friends and have spent a lot of time together. When Diane was in crisis due to her husband's abuse, Kate was always there to help. Once, when Diane had been beaten by her husband and was considering leaving him, Kate flew across the country unasked to pick her up and take her back to their hometown. Diane had not even requested that Kate come to her aid, but Kate believed that going to get her and bring her home would be best under the circumstances.

Diane was, in Kate's words, "dazed and confused" when she arrived, and seemed to need someone to help her make decisions, so Kate did "what needed to be done" in Diane's best interest. The problem was that Diane was not directing her own life, Kate was. Kate rented a U-Haul to move all of Diane's possessions home with them, secretly hoping that this would make Diane not want to go back to her husband. It didn't work: after a few months Diane did decide to go back.

Upon leaving Kate's home to return to Mike, Diane blamed Kate for the problems caused by the rescue. Diane had lost her job and Mike quit his job and gave up their apartment to travel across the country to get Diane to come back to him. Kate was furious that she would be blamed for trying to help Diane. She ended Diane's stay by ordering Diane to "get out of my house!" For Kate, it felt like a slap in the face: "I busted my butt for you and this is the thanks I get!" It took a year for Kate to resolve her anger with Diane.

Diane, of course, had her own reactions to her experiences of that time. She recently told me that during her stay with Kate, after that particular rescue attempt, she felt very alone, even in the midst of her family members' rush to be helpful; finding baby-sitters, paying for college, getting her a car and place to live, none of which Diane asked for.

Apparently, in the flurry of excitement and plans made on Diane's behalf, no one in the family remembered to sit with Diane and listen to what she needed. Indeed, Diane was so lonely for a close emotional connection that she secretly called her husband on the phone every day during her stay because he felt more like an anchor to her than anyone in her family did.

Kate's Decision to Change

Kate didn't realize until much later that, in being helpful to Diane, she was really putting her down and fostering Diane's dependency on herself and on others. Kate assumed that she was a good decision maker, and since Diane sometimes asked for her help, she should help Diane by making decisions for her.

When Kate attempted to make decisions for Diane, Diane initially came up with reasons why she couldn't do whatever it was Kate was suggesting. Undaunted, Kate would think of more solutions to her sister's problems. If Kate suggested she get her college degree, Diane said she didn't have the money for tuition. If Kate gave her the tuition money, Diane claimed she couldn't find baby-sitting during class time, etc., etc. Finally, Diane would wear down and reluctantly go along with Kate's decisions, but secretly resented Kate for controlling her.

Kate thought she was keeping Diane's best interest at heart, but instead of encouraging her sense of herself as a competent decision maker, she was inadvertently fostering Diane's dependency. What Diane needed, instead, was someone to be there for her, to help her do things she asked to have done, to promote her confidence in her own abilities. She needed an anchor.

Since Jackie had been working for some time on becoming an anchor, she tried to encourage Kate to be an anchor to Diane rather than her rescuer. It took Kate a while to see that rescuing Diane wasn't working. As is true for most of us, she had to reach that awareness in her own time. She did so and subsequently accepted the challenge, just as Jackie had done earlier, to work toward becoming an anchor.

TO BE AN ANCHOR

MY FRIEND SARA

In Chapter Three I told you a little about my abuse experience. Now I would like to tell you more about it and about the person who acted as my anchor.

Sara was my roommate at that time, both of us in the same graduate program studying to become psychotherapists. One day I came home from seeing my boyfriend, Joe, and told Sara the awful events of that day: I had told Joe that I planned on dating other men because our relationship wasn't going anywhere. Joe became irrational with rage, blocked my exit from his room, and punched me several times on the head with his fists. He was immediately sorry for his actions and in his remorse allowed me to go home.

Sara reacted to my story calmly but with obvious concern for my well-being. She listened intently to my feelings and plans for safety in case he chose to pursue me, gently asking questions and guiding me to think about the important issues and decisions I faced.

Joe did indeed pursue me. A few short days later he was calling my apartment implying that if I didn't at least talk to him in person, he would make a scene at my apartment, in front of all my neighbors, until I did. Naively, I thought that talking to him would appease him, so I agreed to do so. During that conversation he persuaded me to visit him at his house over the Labor Day holiday, as a friendship effort. I did hope that we could be friends because I really liked a part of him, the nonviolent part. I agreed to visit him. Sara let me know that my decision to see Joe again worried her, but she didn't attempt to rescue me from my decision, nor did she distance from me. She was clearly there for me but worried about my safety nonetheless.

During the Labor Day visit Joe beat me severely. His anger at my dating other men, even though he had agreed we should just be friends, built gradually over the day until it exploded. He proceeded to hit and terrorize me over the next eight hours. He took me into town (he lived in an isolated rural farming area) and left me in the car while he went into his friends' house. I saw my chance and made my escape, frantically running down side streets of this little town looking for a place to hide, finally finding a deep ditch by the roadside. After a few hours in the ditch, when I thought he had given up the search for me, I sneaked back to the friends' house and told them what had happened. They took me in and let me stay there that night.

The next morning I woke up sore all over with a big bruise covering one eye. The first person I called was Sara, because I knew what her response would be. She was calming and matter-of-fact and said she'd pick me up as soon as she could get there. When she arrived I immediately felt better. She helped me think through legal options and when the clerk at the sheriff's department made condescending remarks to me, "Honey, what did you do to make him so mad?" Sara stood up for me. She told the clerk, "Joe chose to assault Susan and nothing she did caused that!" Sara continued to advocate for me with the sheriff, asking questions and insisting on swift action with regard to Joe's arrest.

Most important, Sara treated me with respect, even though my choice to see Joe again was such a poor one. Never once did Sara say "I told you so" or imply that she thought badly of me. I could tell she didn't think badly of me as a person, even though she had known all along that my choice to see Joe again was a dangerous one. Because Sara was able to be my anchor I was able to get through a terrifying and embarrassing time of my life with my self-esteem intact.

A WOMAN WHO IS BEING ABUSED MUST FEEL POWERFUL IN HER ABILITY TO MAKE ADEQUATE DECISIONS IN HER LIFE IF SHE IS TO BREAK FREE OF HER ABUSIVE PARTNER'S CONTROL OVER HER. As a *survivor* of abuse she has strengths which have made her survival possible. Indeed, she is probably very competent in many areas, even though at times she may be unaware of her own abilities. For instance, she might be particularly skilled at prioritizing and balancing a lot of different tasks at once, or acutely attuned to other people's needs, skills which have helped her survive life with a demanding and egocentric partner.

An anchor is a person who supports, empowers, and expands her basic competence. It is a person who helps her focus on her strengths, feelings, and needs, and helps her to feel good about making the safest decisions for herself. In contrast, a rescuer tends to focus on her disabilities and takes over decision making, causing her to lose confidence. A distancer tends to ignore her feelings and needs, leaving her to feel more isolated and that no one cares about her.

An anchor offers her a sense of belonging, a safe relationship in which to heal. In contrast, a distancer offers no connection, therefore, no sense of belonging. Rescuers offer belonging and acceptance on their terms (if you do it my way I will accept you). Rescuer describes a way of being which is overtly controlling and conditional. Distancer describes a way of being which is unaccepting and emotionally removed. Anchor describes a way of being that is accepting, stable, unaggressive, and responsive.

In real life an anchor is powerful only because it sits heavy and grounded at the bottom of a sometimes tumultuous sea. Its cable reaches up to the surface and may be visible as a buoy, a bright-colored bobbing ball—unthreatening, an invitation rather than a threat. An anchor says, "I'm here," but never aggressively controls the ship. Therefore, as an anchor, you remain stationary and ready, listening. As you develop an anchoring relationship, you will find yourself becoming less judgmental, less critical, less directive, accepting. You give up your agendas. You are not an active rescuer, no coast guard or navy, but a lifeline.

ABBY'S ANCHOR

If you are still wondering if an anchor can really have any impact or make a difference, consider the accomplishments of Justine, Abby's anchor.

As the abuse in Abby's marriage worsened, she didn't trust anyone to be there to help her in the way she needed and wanted help. She had gone to family and friends for help before, but they either didn't take her abuse seriously or were too controlling. Her husband had always said that her family was not trustworthy and she began to believe him.

When her cousin Justine, who had previously been distant, began to call Abby just to talk, Abby was cautiously optimistic. It felt really good that Justine cared enough to call, but she wasn't sure if Justine had some other hidden agenda.

As Justine continued her calls, listening and communicating effectively, without judgment, it became clear to Abby that she had no hidden agenda, really did care, and wasn't going to hurt her. Abby gradually began to trust Justine and feel what real trust was like again.

As Abby began to trust Justine more, the lack of trust she had for her husband became more apparent and uncomfortable for her. As she attempted to discuss these concerns with her husband his abuse of her worsened. At the same time, her trust in her cousin was strengthening. When Abby decided to leave her husband, seeing little chance for change in their relationship, Justine was the first person she called for help.

An anchoring relationship teaches trust. Consider the abused woman's situation. The abuse experience might have made her suspicious of anyone wanting to help and support her. Her abusive partner has probably twisted the concept of trust in such a way as to shatter her willingness to trust others. It might be hard for her to fathom that an anchor has no agenda except to care about her. However, it is the very process of learning to trust her anchor which can help an abused woman. Through that relationship she can be reminded what *real* trust is, who is trustworthy, and how to trust someone again or for the first time.

Remember that at first she might not seem to value your anchoring role. Some of the women who came to stay in the shelter I worked in had given up on trust. They had been burned one too many times by their partners, friends, family, and others, and they were bitter.

For many of those women the shelter was the only place they could turn to for help; no one else would help them. At the same time, it was difficult for many of those women to accept that we cared about them. Some women, expecting rejection, would be hostile and rejecting of us from the start. Some women would even test how much we cared about them by going against the rules of the shelter. It would take many of these women a long time before they risked trusting us.

More important still is an anchor's role in helping an abused woman learn to trust herself. Again, through her abusive relationship, she has probably come to question her feelings, decisions, and actions. An anchor gently reminds her of who she is, separate and apart from her abusive partner, who she was before she met him, and who she will always be deep down inside. An anchor can reflect back to an abused woman who she is when she is under her partner's influence, so that she can witness the negative changes within her that have taken place.

Justine, from the previous example, helped Abby learn to trust herself again by "mirroring" or paraphrasing back to Abby what she had said during their phone conversations (more on mirroring in Chapter Five). This had the effect of letting Abby hear herself, what she was saying and feeling, getting to know herself from a different perspective.

Jackie helped Diane trust who she was inside by reminiscing about their childhood and by getting their brothers and sisters together for fun outings. Doing this reminded Diane how happy and free-spirited she was before she met her husband. Then, it was painfully apparent how anxious and withdrawn she had become since her marriage to him.

Typically, for a client in a violent relationship, when I paraphrased back to her what she seemed to be saying to me, she would be appalled to hear how she was coming across. She hadn't realized until then how much she had changed since the abuse began.

If an abused woman can see and hear the different sides

of herself, she can begin to make decisions about who she wants to be. If she chooses her inner self, as opposed to the self which has been defined by her partner, she is on her way toward rediscovering her inherent personality. Through this process of rediscovery she can unlock her own power to make changes in her life. Tapping into this internal power is the only way she will be able to create a life safe and free from an abusive partner. This is the role you choose when you choose to become an anchor.

ARE YOU *ABLE* TO BE HER ANCHOR?

Perhaps at this juncture you are wondering whether or not you are capable of being an anchor for someone. Not everyone is suited to be an anchor.

You may not have the capacity for connectedness she needs. You may discover, painful as it can be, that you don't have the desire or ability to accept her as she is, or the self-control to curtail rescuing or distancing actions which might effectively hinder or harm her in some way. Your relationship with her may be filled with so much hurt or animosity that the amount of work necessary to counteract the layers of pain between you is just not worth it to you. You might recognize your own personality limitations due, perhaps, to your own familial experiences. You might simply not want to devote the time necessary to become and act as anchor for someone.

All of these reasons, and many others, are legitimate. Not all people can be or are needed to be anchors. An anchor relationship is very special and unique to the particular individuals involved. The two most important things, from my point of view, are that you know yourself well enough to know your own limits and limitations, and that you are honest about them with yourself and the woman you care about.

Becoming someone's anchor may be a very natural progression for you out of your increasing awareness and concern for her. If it is not, and you desire it, you may need to make some changes in the way you think, feel, or act, changes which may be difficult to make. In fact, many people can only accomplish these kinds of internal changes when it is more scary and painful *not* to change. Something tragic has to happen before they are catapulted into action.

For some relatives of battered women I have worked with, it was when she showed them her cuts or bruises that they were able to recognize the seriousness of the violence she lived with. Only then were they able to make the changes necessary to help and support her, to be her anchor.

The most difficult part of making personal changes is that it doesn't work if you focus on changing someone else. If you hope that by being an anchor you will guide the battered woman you care about to leave the batterer, or improve her choices of men, or get help for her children, think again. To do this work with such a focus puts you in a position of control. Understandably you might want those outcomes, but practically, you must not focus on them as an agenda. Such an agenda leads to behaviors and attitudes that will alienate her, because they imply that you know what is right for her and that she doesn't. That is the last role to assume with an abused woman if you wish to empower her to help herself.

Your focus as an anchor must be on being the kind of person who connects with others, specifically with the woman you care about. If you make the decision to do that, the rest of this book is designed to guide you, whether you have a lot of changes to make or just a few adjustments in your strategy.

AN ANCHOR'S RESPONSIBILITIES

As you make your choice, always keep in mind you are not responsible for *her* outcome. Even if you follow my suggestions to the letter and she stays with him, you didn't necessarily do something wrong. Even if you choose to do nothing at all and he kills her, you are not at fault for her death. The batterer is.

On the flip side, do not take responsibility for her successes. If she comes to you for help and she ends up leaving her abusive partner, you might conclude that your help *caused* her to leave him. In order to stay out of a position of control over her or her life, you must not take credit for her negative outcomes or responsibility for her successes.

You can and should be responsible for your own changes. Your negative outcomes and successes are often less apparent, but you can get in the habit of looking for them along the way. Jackie, for example, knew that it was time to call me when she was feeling like a failure, knowing that I would help her think of her overall improvements rather than her temporary shortcomings. If you think of it this way you won't be nearly as likely to fall into the trap many friends and family members fall into—hopefulness, disappointment, rejection, emotional distance. If you go into this effort with the goal of saving her, you will be disappointed somewhere along the way. She will be, too.

If you decide to do anchor work, the information contained in this book can help you find your way. Because everyone is different, where you begin the process of becoming an anchor will be unique, as will be the difficulties you face along the way.

For some, making the changes necessary to become an anchor will require a large commitment of time and energy. Others will find that they don't have to make many changes, though they may still need to bridge the distance and get into an anchor position. It is a process, and as such does not occur in neat, sequential stages.

The kinds of changes I'm proposing are not made in a week or a month, or however long it takes for you to read this book. These kinds of changes take time and knowledge, experience and practice. This book will give you the knowledge you need. It will be up to you to practice the suggestions contained in it.

Don't be surprised if there are times when you feel like you are making no progress. You may even consider giving up the work. These feelings are a natural part of any significant personal change. But don't let them stop you, because if you continue working through times of self-doubt and discouragement, you will be rewarded with a sense of confidence and accomplishment, not to mention better relationships.

WHAT'S IN IT FOR ME?

Perhaps you are wondering, can I get anything out of doing this work, in addition to helping the abused woman I care about? Are anchor skills generalizable to all personal relationships, not just those with abused women?

Yes, I think anchor skills are very generalizable. As you practice your anchor skills with others, besides your abused friend or relative, those relationships will be positively affected, too. You can use anchor skills to help you be more helpful toward or closer with anyone. You don't have to act as anchor to everyone in your life, but when you have the anchor skills, you can pull them out to use with anyone you choose, at any time.

Anchor skills are particularly helpful in relationships where blocks to intimacy exist, whatever they might be. If you begin to break down the barriers holding you emotionally separate from others, you receive many rewards. One reward comes when another person begins to accept your attempts at a closer relationship. When this happens, that person may be able to reciprocate and begin to behave more anchorlike with you, encouraging the closeness. You may eventually have a new friend supporting you when you need it, accepting you for who you are.

You will discover things about yourself through your deeper relationships with others that you would never discover were you to remain closed up within yourself. We are social beings. It is only through relationships with others that many aspects of our selves are brought to the surface. The closer you become to someone else, the more of yourself you can discover.

I can't project what your personal discoveries will be because you are unique. I can tell you, if you are open to see it, that you will uncover rich and surprising qualities which have been lying dormant, waiting for you to become someone's anchor.

ARE YOU READY?

The following are criteria which will help you decide if you're ready to do anchor work. Keep them in mind as you read the rest of this book:

1. You know that a woman is experiencing abuse in her relationship, and you see it as dangerous and painful for her.

2. You can see specific areas of distance in your relationship with her and you want to be closer to her emotionally.

3. You are ready to focus on your own changes, not hers.

4. You realize that you can make a difference in her life.

5. You believe that the changes you make will benefit you, too.

CHAPTER FIVE

⟨✦⟩

To Act as an Anchor Before She Asks for Help

What does it mean to *act* as an anchor for the woman you care about? It means that you can behave like an anchor before you feel at all like one. You can practice the skills an anchor uses with the understanding that those skills will eventually become part of who you are. Then you will *be* an anchor.

THE MOST IMPORTANT INGREDIENT IN AN ANCHORING RELATIONSHIP IS TRUST. Indeed, the only way the battered woman you care about will ever share her story with you or ask for your help is if she trusts you not to harm her, and to accept her as she is.

The other side to this is that she probably won't completely trust you to accept and not hurt her unless you know how to communicate with her. TRUST DEPENDS ON EFFECTIVE COMMUNICATION. So, one way to practice being an anchor for the woman you're concerned about is to work toward better communication. An anchor is only as useful to a boat as the effectiveness of the rope which ties them together. The floundering ship needs to "trust" that the lifeline won't break or pull her so close she can't "be" a ship. That is where communication comes in.

THE DRUDGERY PART

This is the most difficult part of the process of becoming an anchor. You will be trying on new behaviors which might be very uncomfortable at first. Furthermore, you probably won't be rewarded for a while, sometimes a long while. Jackie found this part to be absolute drudgery! As a very goal-oriented person, she found this work too intangible. She just had to trust that I knew what I was talking about (especially difficult for a control freak like Jackie to do), grit her teeth, and do it! There are rewards down the road. You probably won't be able to see them yet, but they are there. For now, however, you will need to operate on faith.

Be aware that the woman you care about may *never* come to you for help no matter how hard you try or how well you perform the techniques outlined in this book. She and her partner are outside the realm of your control. What he does to her and what she chooses to do about it is, ultimately, up to them. You can only focus on your own behavior and hope that it is enough to influence her in a positive way. I must reiterate, because this principle is so crucial to becoming an anchor: YOU ARE NOT RESPONSIBLE FOR THE BATTERER'S BEHAVIOR, OR FOR HIS VICTIM'S ACTIONS, OR LACK OF ACTION. YOU *ARE* RESPONSIBLE FOR YOUR OWN DECISIONS AND BEHAVIOR.

Try to remember that developing new emotional connections with someone is a process. This process doesn't always have a clear beginning or end. The nature of it is sometimes cyclical, and as such, you may find yourself needing to return over and over to basic concepts in this book. Expect to take two steps forward and one step back. Try to see your overall improvement rather than focus too heavily on temporary setbacks. There is no perfect or right way to accomplish these changes. As I have said before, you will find your own way.

Jackie was too hard on herself, focusing on how far she had to go in her journey to becoming an experienced anchor; she failed to recognize how very far she had come. Only after other women friends began searching her out for help did Jackie realize the other benefits of being an anchor. As she was able to give to others and friends told her how much they appreciated her gifts of self, she began to feel more calm and self-directed, at peace with herself, fully connected.

ESTABLISHING CONTACT

If you are not already talking *regularly* with your battered friend or family member, it is time to get that going. Regularity is a key to trust: not only does regular communication open doors, it signifies that you are reliable, you will not go away. But talking with a battered woman can be a task in itself since her abusive partner will usually try to isolate her from others, especially potential anchors! You may need to be very creative in finding a regular avenue through which to reach her.

In Jackie's attempts to reconnect with Diane she first

had to get past the fear involved in reaching out to her sister. They had never been close emotionally and she feared Diane might be suspicious of her reasons for calling just to chat. It was a big risk for Jackie to call because she was, in effect, challenging long-held family roles, in particular, her own role as distancer.

When Jackie decided to put her fears aside and contact Diane she had difficulty:

> In the beginning it was hard to reach Diane by phone. Many times Diane and her husband were there (I later found out) but Diane didn't answer because she was so anxious about her husband's reaction to the phone call, that she let the machine get it. When she did answer and Mike was home, she was guarded and superficial. Finally I realized that the only way to have a private conversation with Diane was to call on the one day she was off of work and Mike wasn't there to screen the call.

Jackie's fears were not realized and Diane responded happily to her calls. This encouraged Jackie and she began to call regularly, once a week, so that Diane would come to expect her call.

CONSISTENCY IS VERY IMPORTANT TO THE DEVELOPMENT OF TRUST, AND THEREFORE TO CLOSER CONNECTIONS. If a person knows what to expect and when to expect it from you they can begin to feel safer within your relationship. This is especially important for battered women because they don't experience much safety or consistency in their life.

It is not necessary that you call on the telephone in order to connect with the woman you care about. Talking in person, writing letters, E-mail, or any other way you can

think of to communicate with her is fine. THE IMPOR-
TANT THING TO CONSIDER IS HER PRIVACY AND
SAFETY. Try to contact her so that her partner is not
likely to see or hear your conversation. Then, respect her
wishes on how and when future talks should take place.
She may not tell you directly that she's uncomfortable that
he will overhear your conversation, but you can listen
carefully to what she does say to get a sense of how comfortable she is talking with you. If she seems distracted or
upset when you speak to her, respect her privacy without
assuming you know what's bothering her. You can always
considerately ask, "Is this a bad time for you to talk?" If she
says "yes," you can always tell her that you would like to
talk to her again soon. And, if she responds positively to
that, be sure to contact her again. If, after several times of
contacting her, she seems uncomfortable with your efforts,
you can say something to the effect of, "I was hoping we
could begin to talk to each other more regularly, but it
seems like you're not really interested in that right now. Is
that right?" Honor what she says in answer. Your effort, in
itself, will show her that you are there for her should she
decide that she needs help or support from someone in the
future.

Please remember, these example statements are my words,
not yours. It is very important that you say only what you
can believe and in your own words. It may feel terribly uncomfortable, but that is natural if you are changing the way
you behave in a relationship. It would be nice if you could
feel completely comfortable with your new behavior before
you try it on, but that's not likely to happen. You usually
have to practice something new many times before it becomes comfortable and second nature.

It would also be nice if you could feel closer to her first

so that establishing contact would be easier. The change I'm talking about doesn't often happen spontaneously. We *make* it happen by changing our own behavior. ACTION OFTEN PRECEDES CHANGE, RATHER THAN FOLLOWING IT. If you are biding your time, hoping for change to happen spontaneously, you could be in for a long wait.

It is easy to underestimate the difficulty in contacting, for the first time, a battered woman you care about. It sounds so simple to just pick up the phone and call her. But it may not be. If reconnecting seems to be an insurmountable hurdle, other complex and unconscious issues could be operating that are keeping you at a distance from her. Consider seeking the help of a good professional counselor/therapist who can help you unlock these mysteries so as to free you to be able to connect.

USING GOOD COMMUNICATION SKILLS

During those awkward initial contacts, what should you talk about? The answer to that question is any subject about which you can be open (noncritical and nonjudgmental) to her perspective. You could talk about your children, her work, the yard work, the weather. It isn't necessary that you talk about complicated, deep personal topics to show her that you can be trusted not to hurt or judge her. You can go a long way toward this goal by using some basic communication skills.

When Jackie first began contacting Diane, she shied away from talking about Diane's husband altogether, because she knew that it would be difficult not to express her negative feelings about him (and consequently about Diane's decision to be with him). Jackie chose to connect with Diane during those first phone conversations by throwing out topics completely unrelated to Diane's abuse (the weather, work, children), even though the abuse was common knowledge in the family at that point. She felt it would be the least threatening way to begin establishing trust.

The object of your effort is to build trust so that the battered woman will come to you. BE PATIENT. THE ESTABLISHMENT OF TRUST CAN'T BE FORCED. You must plant the seeds and hope they grow. To force or push would be the opposite of what would encourage her trust in you. You are there to try to hear and understand her, not to solve her problems for her or even to form an opinion about what she is saying. For her to eventually be able to tell the stories of her experience to one who can hear and is trying to understand her is helpful in itself.

The following communication skills are basic, yet key to any effective communication effort. If you use them when you are with your battered friend or relative, you will hear and understand things she says which you may never have heard the same way before.

Expect that she might be uncomfortable with your new anchor behavior for awhile and may, therefore, continue to react to you in the same old ways that she always has. Human beings are pretty stubborn about changing long-held roles. That is what you are doing, changing your role with her. She may be actively angry or upset by this change. It may seem for a while that anchor skills are actually working against your relationship with her. She may distance from you. You may feel, at this point, like giving it up. Try to keep in mind that her strong reaction (often seen as digging in her heels or grasping at straws, anything she can do to elicit your old way of reacting to her) to your change may actually mean that what you are doing is working! Don't discount her reactions as insignificant, yet do try to see her reactions for what they mean, rather than how they appear superficially. Try to give it more time and look for small changes in your relationship which signal improved closeness. Change of this sort happens in small increments, not by leaps and bounds. Your new behavior and subsequent role will take getting used to, for both of you.

The transition toward anchor may be smoother for both of you if you explain your attempts to change (always focusing on your feelings, your changes, not on how you hope she will change in response to you). Say something like, "I'm trying to be a better listener and get closer to people I care about. You're one of those people I care about, so I just wanted to let you know that I might seem a little different in the way I act." You might even go further to solicit her help in your change: "Could you let me know if I do something which makes you uncomfortable?" This opens up conversation and lets her know that you value her feelings about even uncomfortable topics.

As in learning any new skill, you can expect to make mistakes when learning new communication skills. It's O.K. to make mistakes. Try not to panic when you do. Most conversations are not the final opportunity to talk with someone. Use your mistakes to help you plan what to say (and what not to say) the next time and make that next conversation happen.

PRINCIPLES OF GOOD COMMUNICATION

1. USE OPEN BODY LANGUAGE—The way you hold your body during a conversation with an abused woman (or anyone else for that matter) can communicate a

lot to her. If your body is physically closed, arms crossed at your chest and legs crossed at the knee, and you are looking at everything other than her face, you will be sending the message that you are not very open to listening to what she has to say. If, on the other hand, you sit or stand facing her, regularly look her in the eye when she talks, and keep arms and legs relaxed and uncrossed, you are expressing through body language your desire to hear whatever she has to say to you. This is a simple yet often neglected aspect of good communication. If you don't *look* like a person who wants to hear what she has to say, she probably won't risk saying much to you, particularly the uncomfortable abuse stories. Remember, if this suggestion sounds too premeditated, that you are *acting*: the behavior comes first, the internal changes will follow.

2. BE HONEST WITH HER AND YOURSELF—She won't trust you unless you are honest with her. I don't mean the type of brutal honesty which confronts her with feelings or opinions you might have which she didn't ask for or desire. I mean the type of honest answer to a direct question which considers her feelings in how it is framed. If she asks you, for example, "Do you like my husband?" An example of the brutally honest answer would be, "That jerk! Who could like a wife-beater like him?" The more carefully framed answer would be, "I don't like the way he hurts you, but, then again, I have not seen the other sides of him which you tell me are nice." Both answers are honest, but the latter considers the feelings of the woman with whom you're speaking while the first is more a raw expression of one's own needs. If your needs are to vent your feelings about her abusive partner, for instance, you can do that with someone who is not so emotionally connected to

him as she. Furthermore, it's safest to assume that if she doesn't ask you a question directly, she likely doesn't yet want your input, especially in uncomfortable, personal areas.

3. OPEN EARS, SHUT MOUTH—You can't be listening when you are talking. And when you are trying to put yourself in a position to hear about an uncomfortable topic like physical abuse, it is especially important not to talk too much. Try to focus on what your friend or family member is saying rather than on yourself or what you have to say. Be thoughtful about what you do say. Try to think before you talk. When in doubt as to the right thing to say, DON'T SAY ANYTHING, JUST LISTEN. This can feel very uncomfortable. Most people don't like silences in conversations and fill in with chatter when it occurs. Resist this urge. It is during silences when a lot of connecting can happen.

4. ASK HER TO CLARIFY WHAT YOU DON'T UNDERSTAND—Try to understand not just the words she speaks but what she is attempting to convey to you; the meaning between the lines. This doesn't mean you should try to read her mind or second-guess her. It does mean that you can ask questions to help you understand more clearly what she is trying to convey. If she says, for example, "I've been really down lately," you can clarify with, "How so?" or "What do you mean by down?"

Before a battered women tells someone that she is being abused, she will often say things that are clues to that fact. By dropping hints she can foresee how the listener will handle the "awful truth." She wonders whether or not you will hear her clues at all. She also wonders whether or not you will somehow discount her experiences if you do hear about them. For example, if your battered friend or relative tells you her husband has a Jekyll-and-Hyde personality, and you don't comment on that statement or you, in your discomfort, take the ball away from her ("I feel like Jekyll and Hyde myself sometimes"), she probably won't share the more painful information she holds. If, on the other hand, you ask her to clarify her clue, "What do you mean, a Jekyll-and-Hyde personality?" she is likely to trust that she can share more with you. So, for you to clarify with an abused woman what you think she is trying to say will help her to feel heard and validated, and ultimately that she can trust you to tell you more.

5. BE A MIRROR—Another way to clarify what you heard your friend or relative say is by reflecting her statements back to her. You can restate, using your own words, what she has just told you. For example, if she tells you she misses her husband and wants to go back to him, you can mirror back to her, "You sound like you are feeling lonely and wish you were back with your husband. Is that right?" She can correct you if you misunderstood something she said.

Both mirroring and clarifying have the advantage of helping her to feel control over her side of the conversation. It also lets her know that you are *really* listening and trying to understand her; you're not assuming you know better than she what she means to say. You can bet she doesn't get that kind of respect within her relationship with her abusive partner, so she'll really appreciate it from you.

Mirroring her statements can also help her see inside herself, get in touch with her own instincts and feelings, who she really is apart from his loyal wife or girlfriend. Those parts of her old self are the parts she has probably buried in her futile attempts to keep him happy with her. Those are the parts of her you might have enjoyed before she met him.

Be very careful not to use this mirroring technique to subtly manipulate what she *means* to say toward what you would *like* her to say. Instead, use it to try to discover what she is trying to say between the lines. You are mirroring so as to understand her better, not so you can control what she is feeling or thinking.

6. SPEAK ONLY FOR YOURSELF—Within your relationship with your battered friend or relative be careful to speak from your own perspective, and not *for* her. You can let her know what you feel, believe, and observe without giving her advice, without telling her how she should feel or think, and without judging her (refer to Chapter Six for more discussion on giving advice and on judging her). There can be a fine line between expressing your own feelings and beliefs and being advising, controlling, or judgmental. You may need to pay close attention to your communication style with her to determine which you tend to do.

When you first begin connecting with your abused friend or relative it might be most effective to express only your feelings and observations, not your beliefs. It is very tricky to express beliefs without advising, controlling, or judging. In addition, many battered women are very sensitive to being advised, controlled, and judged, having been smothered by their partners' beliefs. Expressing only your feelings and observations for a while will probably work best to connect with her, e.g., "I *feel* afraid when you tell me about how your husband explodes" or "I *notice* that you're not at the gym as much as you used to be" rather than "I *believe* it is wrong for a husband to treat his wife the way yours treats you."

A technique which will help you stay on the side of expressing your own feelings is using "I" statements. Try to think about statements before you say them and begin them with "I." This will help you frame what you have to say from your own perspective. Notice how often you begin statements with, "You . . ." If you tend to make "you" statements, you might have a tendency to try to control her—"*I* feel sorry that you are struggling to find a good job" versus "*You* need to apply for a job at my company. They're hiring."

Be especially careful not to try to tell her more than she has said about how she *should* feel or think. The quickest way to alienate someone is to try to tell them what they should be thinking or feeling, as in, "*You* don't really love him anymore, you are just tied to him financially." Or, "*You* must despise him for what he did to you." Instead, you could say, "*I'm* wondering about your true feelings for him. How do you feel?" Or, "*I* wonder how his behavior must make you feel. *I* know I'm furious at him when he treats you that way." By beginning your statements with "I" you are owning your feelings and thoughts, and taking yourself out of a control position with the woman you are speaking with.

7. SHARE YOUR "SECRETS" WITH HER—If and when you are able, and it is appropriate for you to be vulnerable with the woman you care about, she will be encouraged to be vulnerable back. Rarely do people spill their guts to those who seem to have no problems of their

own. Like anyone else, battered women tend to confide in people who are willing to share bits of their own less-than-perfect lives. It was when Jackie shared problems she was working on in her own marriage that Diane first began to really confide in Jackie about the abuse she was experiencing with Mike.

I am not talking here about looking to your abused friend or relative as your anchor or counselor. Nor am I talking about taking over conversations so that your problems are the primary topic of discussion. She probably has little enough energy to give to her own survival and problems, she won't have enough to give to yours. What I am talking about here is a general acknowledgment that you have problems, too.

8. ASK OPEN-ENDED QUESTIONS—How are you? How was it when you were with him? What happened last night? How does it feel without him? These are all examples of open-ended questions you might ask an abused woman you care about. Do you want to leave him? Do you like school? Did you see him last night? These are examples of yes/no questions.

Open-ended questions tend to open up the conversation rather than close it down because they ask for broader opinion or general input, feelings or beliefs rather than only a yes or no. When asked an open-ended question, an abused woman is not as limited in her response. She has more control over her reaction than if she is asked a yes/no question.

Of course yes/no questions are a necessary ingredient in conversations. Some people, however, tend to overuse them and underuse open-ended questions. Try to notice which types of questions you use most often. Your connec-

tion with your abused friend or relative may be strength-
ened by your adding more open-ended questions to your
repertoire.

EXAMPLES OF ANCHORS' CONVERSATIONS

Anchor #1:   How was your holiday? (Open-ended
             question)

Friend: Terrible. I left Ed. I was a fool to believe
             his promises before. This time I'm never go-
             ing back.

Anchor #1:   So, you're feeling foolish? (Mirroring)

Friend: Right! I've always been too dependent
             on men.

Anchor #1:   What do you mean, dependent? (Clarifying)

Friend: I've never made my own decisions. I look to
             men to do that for me.

Anchor #1:   I tend to be too dependent on some people
             myself. (Sharing secrets)

Friend: You do?

Anchor #1:   Yes, and I end up feeling resentful and angry
             when I do it. (Speaking for yourself)

             ————

Anchor #2:   Hi! How are you since you moved away
             from John? (Open-ended question)

Sister: Well, I moved back in with him and things
             are going great.

Anchor #2:   So things are going good between you and
             John? (Mirroring)

Sister: Yes. He said he'd go to counseling with
             me and promised he wouldn't hit me again.
             I think he means it this time. At least I
             hope so.

Anchor #2:   You sound hopeful that he'll follow through
             on his promises this time. Are you? (Mirror-
             ing and Clarifying)

Sister: Well, I realize that he has made these
             promises before. And, to be honest, I'm not
             sure that he'll follow through this time ei-
             ther. I just needed to try one more time.

             ———

Anchor #3:   How was your date with Dave last weekend?
             (Open-ended question)

Coworker: It didn't go the way I thought it would.

Anchor #3:   How so? (Open-ended question and
             Clarifying)

Coworker: He blew up at me in the restaurant for no
             reason.

Anchor #3:   What do mean, "blew up"? (Clarifying)

Coworker: He slammed his fist on the table, yelled at
             me to stop nagging at him, and stomped out
             of the restaurant. I felt so embarrassed. I still
             don't know what I did to cause him to act
             that way.

Anchor #3: I noticed you called in sick yesterday. (Speaking for yourself)

Coworker: Yeah. I just felt bad after what happened.

Anchor #3: That was really embarrassing for you, huh? (Mirroring) I think I would feel embarrassed if that happened to me! (Speaking for yourself)

Coworker: You would?

Anchor #3: Yes. My dad used to fly off the handle at nothing when my friends from high school were over. I wanted to melt into the woodwork when he did that. I thought it was my fault but figured out as I got older that he had the problem, not me. (Sharing secrets)

KEEP AFTER IT!

These basic skills are harder to use than they look. Many people work on them for months before getting the hang of it, so don't give up quickly. To speed up the process, practice using these skills with other people you know. It certainly won't hurt your other relationships to do so. It can take quite a long time for these tools to work in establishing a better connection with the abused woman you care about. Be patient. If you are persistent in your honest attempts at reconnecting with your friend or family member, she is likely to reciprocate eventually; that is, if physically free to do so. And if you make a mistake and dominate one conversation, try again. Don't give up on yourself or her. You might even apologize for talking too much.

Remember that she might be living like a prisoner of war, only she happens to love her captor. This factor puts very real limits on how free she is to respond to your attempts to connect with her. She might want desperately to connect with you, too, but may not be doing so out of fear of what her partner may do to her.

ASKING HER SENSITIVE QUESTIONS

Be particularly careful to use the communication skills discussed in this chapter when asking your friend or relative sensitive questions. For instance, at some point when you feel close to her you might deem it appropriate to ask if she has been abused by her partner. If you do ask, be sure to avoid blaming, critical, or judgmental remarks, such as, "You aren't the type to let a guy abuse you, are you?" or "What did you do to him?" You will probably need to shy away from stigmatizing terms like "abuse," "battering," or even "violence." Battered women I've known (myself included) have tended to use those terms to describe *other* women's lives, not theirs. They don't usually think of themselves or their partners in those terms and might resent it if you refer to them in such a way.

So, how do you approach the battered woman you care about with a sensitive question like, "Are you being abused by your husband/boyfriend?" First, speak for yourself. Try to talk about your own feelings toward her: "I'm worried about you." Then you can go on to explain your worry. "Every few months, I notice you come to work with a bruise on a different part of your body and you've mentioned that your husband has a bad temper." Finally, you can ask the question, "Is your husband hurting you?" Be sure to let her respond (or not) fully (open ears, shut mouth), and follow up, keeping in mind the other principles I discuss in this chapter.

JACKIE'S COMMUNICATION LESSONS

Jackie felt very uncomfortable at first when she began talking to Diane in a different way. She had always been quick to give her opinions and advice to others whom, she believed, could use it. She really meant well but her way of communicating tended to close down the other person and push them away, not open them up and draw them nearer. Indeed, when she talked to Diane over the phone during her early attempts at forging a new relationship, she had to write down and refer to a list of dos and don'ts to remind herself of good communication phrasing of certain questions and statements she needed. Jackie began holding her tongue a lot, asking more open-ended questions like, "What happened?" or "How did that make you feel?" instead of "What did he do to you?" She stopped giving advice and opinions off the top of her head. Instead, she focused on Diane and what Diane was trying to say (or sometimes trying *not* to say). She began clarifying what she didn't understand and tried to speak for herself more often. She was really quite shocked when these few skills began to work, and work quickly. One day her work paid off in a big way. In her own words:

> Before I tried being an anchor Diane used to complain about never doing anything fun on the weekends; she was tired from working long hours at her job. I used to

urge her to get a regular job with weekends off, so she
and her husband could have more fun and time to work
on their marriage, which seemed a mess to me. How can
you fix anything if you're not together very much? I
would think to myself. In response to my urging Diane
would give a list of reasons (which is what she always
did when I pushed her to do something she didn't want
to do) why she couldn't do what I had suggested. I came
away from those discussions with the impression that
she was lazy and just liked to complain.

One day I decided to share with her some of my own
marital problems and got a different response. I told her
that because my husband was working a lot of hours, we
were only together on Sundays and somehow always
managed to get in a fight on that one day we were together. That was all it took. Diane began opening up to
me. She said Mike never wanted to do anything fun on
Sunday. The few times he did, if their daughter was a
little fussy, he would go ballistic because Diane couldn't
control the child. After a couple of outings it just wasn't
worth it. Staying home was awful, too, because all Mike
did was drink and continually remark how she had
messed up their lives when she last left him to go stay
with her meddling sister Kate.

This was a great day for me because it was the most
Diane had ever opened up about her real life. Just three
months before we had a superficial relationship. Now
things were changing, all because I followed a few communication guidelines, slowed down and tried to think
instead of just react to her.

After about three months of practice the initial communication skills became more comfortable for Jackie to use,
and Diane was sharing a little more with each passing conversation. Jackie was even able to work into being more of
a mirror, reflecting some of what Diane said back to her.

But that was longer in coming. Most important, Jackie's regular telephone calls to Diane were paying off. Diane was learning that Jackie cared for her enough to call regularly and listen.

ANSWERS TO QUESTIONS YOU MIGHT HAVE

When I try to use my new communication skills to speak with my friend she seems uncomfortable and always switches the subject away from her problems with her abusive boyfriend, even when she was the one who brought up that subject.

When you change the way you communicate with someone, that person isn't likely to respond right away with their own change. People hold on to old ways of interacting for a long time sometimes, even in the face of others' changes. Give your friend time to trust you with her story. Don't push her into talking about things which are obviously uncomfortable, but keep an ear open for when she does give you clues that she is ready to talk about her abuse.

Also keep in mind that there are probably events happening in her life, out of your awareness, which may be keeping her from reciprocating your efforts toward closeness. Understanding that can give you the patience you will need to keep working toward a closer connection with her.

What is the difference between mirroring and analyzing?

Mirroring is simply restating, using different words, what the person to whom you are speaking just said to you. Analyzing is using your own expertise and judgment to offer insights to what the person is telling you of their experience. Let a counselor who is trained at analysis do the analyzing for your loved one. You are not trained to analyze her problems and could cause her harm if you try. Example responses:

Abused Woman: I'm so tired of my husband's excuses. I can't take it anymore. I'm going to file for divorce tomorrow.

Analysis: After years of blaming yourself for your husband's irresponsibility you have developed enough self-esteem to recognize the limits of your control over his behavior and you are taking back control over your own life.

Mirroring: You sound as if you have had enough of your husband's explanations and you've decided to divorce him.

I don't believe in divorce. By being an anchor for my sister am I encouraging her to divorce her husband?

If you are using the principles described in this book you are simply listening to her, how she feels and what she wants to do or not. You are not deciding anything for her. The only thing you are encouraging her to do is to feel good about herself again and to stay safe.

Jackie also struggled with this issue when she was trying to decide how to help Diane. For moral reasons she didn't believe in divorce. But it seemed that by becoming an anchor for Diane she might be encouraging the breakup of her sister's marriage. Jackie believed that "for better or for worse" was a marriage commitment that could not be broken. However, after learning more about the nature of domestic violence and what her sister was really going through in her abusive marriage, Jackie began to see a limit to "for better or for worse."

In a real marriage, both partners must have a true desire for change and take responsibility for their own part in the problems before there can be improvement. Mike, however, had no desire to change. He was quite comfortable continuing his control and abuse of Diane. Their marriage lacked two critical ingredients: safety and mutuality.

Jackie ultimately concluded that divorce was sometimes acceptable as a means for someone to escape a dangerous, hurtful relationship. She began to see that for some women "for better or for worse" is tantamount to "for better or for death." Even if change is possible, a woman in such a relationship may not live long enough to see it improve. Jackie also learned that in her role as anchor she shouldn't attempt to make decisions for Diane. Being an anchor for Diane is about helping her talk about her life, share her feelings, and recognize the choices available to her. But hardest of all, being an anchor is about supporting a loved one whose decisions you may not agree with.

CHAPTER SIX

—∞∞∞—

To Act as
an Anchor When
She Comes to You

Perhaps you are beginning to see that it is truly possible to help the abused woman you care about, that you really *can* make a difference! Hopefully, if she has not already done so, your abused friend or relative will begin to trust you with her secret and come to you for help or support. If she is not yet confiding in you and you feel you are actively using the skills discussed so far, try to be patient. Trust takes time to develop.

THERE IS EXCITEMENT AND ANXIETY

The woman you care about finally shares her story with you or even asks directly for your help. What do you do next? You may still just be learning how to *act* like an anchor, and not yet feel like one. You might be feeling a mix of emotions, excitement that the communication skills are working to establish trust in your relationship with her, and worry that you will somehow mess up the progress which is occurring.

You might be noticing yourself making a lot of mistakes in your use of the communication skills you learned in Chapter Five. Take heart; you'll make a lot more mistakes before this is all over. That's O.K. No one (except you maybe) expects perfection. The important thing is that you try, and keep trying.

It is also important that you recognize that if an abused woman comes to you with her abuse story it is because *she chose you*, it wasn't just happenstance. Whether you realize it or not she has been testing you, watching how you handle yourself when she shares seemingly insignificant information about herself and small clues to her abuse. She has seen that you are to be trusted, that you will listen. If she is sharing her abuse story with you it is time to congratulate yourself.

WHEN DIANE CAME TO JACKIE FOR HELP

To Jackie, the six months that had passed since she began to work toward becoming Diane's anchor felt like six years, but her use of the communication skills she had learned was becoming more natural. She was also beginning to view her own discomfort with trying on new behavior as a sign that she was accomplishing positive changes for herself. She could now see that the small changes she was making would eventually combine to produce big results, so she was, at times, more patient with herself than she had been.

One day, just as Jackie had hoped for many months, Diane called her and asked for help. Diane said that her husband had beaten her the night before and that she was planning to leave him. She asked if she and their five-year-old daughter, Beth, could come and stay with Jackie. Jackie wholeheartedly agreed, trying to keep her elation at the news of Diane's leaving down to a mild excitement.

With Diane and Beth's arrival came a host of unexpected experiences for Jackie. In her own words . . .

I was so excited that Diane had left Mike and had come to stay with me. All my work was paying off! The reality, however, soon set in. I was suddenly around her and Beth twenty-four hours a day at a time when they were experiencing tremendous turmoil. The first couple of days after Diane arrived at my house were the most emotional; she cried at the drop of a hat, was frantic, angry, and so sad. She was finally letting out the flood of emotions that had been building inside her for years. She seemed to need to just talk, cry, and think. She needed quiet time to reflect on her feelings and circumstances. There wasn't enough of that at my house, however, between the children and other people in the family coming in and out. It was an obvious strain for her to hold herself together when other people would come over. I felt the desire to push everything and everyone else aside so that I could concentrate on Diane's tremendous needs. I was very tempted to change my whole anchor strategy, now that she was openly looking to me for advice and support. I really wanted to jump in and start directing her in "positive" directions. I had to slow myself down, talk to Susan a lot, and remember to continue on in the same manner which had worked so far. Diane trusted me now and I didn't want to mess that up.

After the first couple of days Diane began to talk more about the gory details of the abuse she experienced. That was really hard for me to hear, but I forced myself to listen. I had particular difficulty remembering not to agree with her when she would speak badly of Mike. I wanted so desperately to be a good anchor to Diane, always keeping in mind that she might very well return to Mike. I was also beginning to worry about our safety, since Mike knew where we lived and might come looking for Diane. It was such a relief when she agreed with me that it was safest for her and Beth to move out of my house and into her own place. I think it was just as much a relief to her, too. She needed her own space, a place to begin to heal.

During those first weeks after Diane's arrival, Jackie struggled with herself to not control Diane. It was very tempting for Jackie to want to take credit for Diane's success. After all, she had worked hard to connect with Diane for six months and she felt rewarded when Diane actually left her husband to come to stay with her! She had to remind herself of what we had discussed earlier—that she could not accept responsibility for Diane's successes, just as she should not blame herself for Diane's failures. Indeed, she had to remember that Diane's leaving her marriage was neither a success nor a failure. It was simply Diane's decision, which Jackie would need to honor.

At the same time, Jackie was very surprised by how difficult it was to be around Diane. She was so excited that Diane chose to stay with her, she didn't consider how intense the emotions of a woman and her child would be when they had just left their nightmare. She was frantic to find out the right way to handle her sister's crisis and was relieved to discover that she should just continue doing what she had been doing.

Even after Diane moved out of Jackie's home and into her own, it became increasingly uncomfortable for Jackie to be so close to the chaos surrounding Diane's marriage, and she found she was emotionally distancing herself from Diane as she had done before beginning the anchor work. "It feels like I'm always moving two steps forward and one step back," Jackie said to me one time in dismay. She had to be reminded that progress can be very slow and incremental. Patience and self-awareness are key. She discovered the need to remind herself over and over, and for many months subsequent, that she wanted a close relationship with her sister regardless of what circumstances Diane was facing. Jackie also had to remember that hers was not just an altruistic effort. She was changing in ways which were benefiting her a great deal in her other relationships. As ambivalent as she had again become about continuing her work toward a closer relationship with Diane, she ultimately decided not to turn back.

HELPING YOUR FRIEND OR RELATIVE WHEN SHE COMES TO YOU

First, a word of caution: if an abused woman you care about comes to you with her story or for help, you may regress and fall into old patterns of rescuing or distancing. The closer you get and the more you know, the more you will have to fight your own demons.

You will probably feel most frustrated when she is intimately involved with her abusive partner. This feeling naturally arises out of your concern for her safety. But when she is with him it is especially tricky to act as an anchor for her and not get into the advice or control trap. It probably seems abundantly clear to you what would solve all her problems—leave him! But you may (rightly) have a sense that to say this to her will alienate her from you. Neither of you would be better off, and you would each be resentful of the other; you, that she didn't accept your heartfelt advice, and she, that you would give that particular advice.

If she is separated from him it is difficult to keep from siding against him or getting overly involved in *your* plans for her life. You may feel so relieved that she is away and seemingly safe from him that you forget what it means to be her anchor. You may find yourself telling her whom she should date (to keep from getting into this mess again), or how to handle her money (so as not to become dependent upon another abuser like the last), or how happy you are that she finally came to her senses and left the jerk! You may alternately find yourself distancing from her. Perhaps you feel that she doesn't need an anchor once she has left him. Or, that her needs have become so consuming that you are being drained of too much energy.

Whether or not she is currently with him, to be an effective anchor you must maintain a difficult balance between supporting her and reflecting reality. You must be honest with her while at the same time carefully choosing what to share and what not to share of your own opinions and feelings. She will need to tell her abuse stories over and over before solutions to her problems begin to form in her mind. For her to go *through* her emotional pain, rather than around it, will help her get stronger. It can be frustrating to hear the same stories repeatedly, and you may feel a strong urge to do something actively to help her. Even if you are fighting a tendency to rescue, there is a time when taking direct action without her direction is indicated (discussed later in this chapter); however, first I will discuss how it is usually best to respond when an abused woman shares her story with you.

PRINCIPLES FOR BEING OF HELP

The principles listed here can be applied when a battered woman shares her abuse story with you, whether or not she is asking for your help or support and whether or not she is with her abusive partner. As you read these, refer regularly to the communication skills in the previous chapter. They are the basic elements on which these subsequent skills are built. A good sign that you are utilizing the skills as intended is if you and the woman you care about are growing closer emotionally and she is beginning to open up and share some painful experiences with you.

1. BELIEVE HER. A battered woman can hardly believe what she is experiencing. She really isn't sure that anyone else will believe it, even if she tells it as she sees it. Most battered women don't lie or exaggerate their abuse. On the contrary, as I discussed in Chapter Two, most minimize the extent of it. However, under the extreme stress of a beating some women may have spotty recollections of their experience, so that what she tells you of the violent events may not be completely factual. What she is telling you is what *she* experienced as reality, not as an objective participant but as a victim of trauma. FOR YOU TO ACCEPT AND VALIDATE HER REALITY IS WHAT'S IMPORTANT, NOT DETERMINING WITH PRECISION THE FACTS OF THE CASE. You can do this by telling her that you believe her story, her feelings and perceptions. To do so is crucial to her mind's clarity, her self-esteem, and the deepening of your relationship with her.

2. TAKE HER ABUSE SERIOUSLY. Almost 30 percent of all female homicide victims in the United States during

1992 (1,414 women) were known to have been killed by their husbands, former husbands, boyfriends, or former boyfriends.[1] Your battered friend or family member's life is in danger whether she is married to, living with, or dating her batterer. She is also in danger after she leaves him. Many batterers stalk and assault (and some kill!) their victims after their victims have left the relationship. For you to believe this and take it seriously may mean that she (and others who may be of critical help to her) can begin to see the dangerousness in her circumstances, if she doesn't already, and act accordingly.

You can show her that you are taking her abuse experience seriously by: listening carefully to what she tells you, not minimizing her abuse yourself, and not passively agreeing with her or others when they minimize the seriousness of her abuse experience.

If you have difficulty with this area refer back to Chapter Two and consider your own preconceptions about domestic violence before moving ahead with anchor work.

3. REMAIN NEUTRAL, DON'T TAKE SIDES. Taking sides, even if it is her side, will only place her in a position in which she'll eventually have to choose between you and her partner. She will usually choose him. Then, she will either further minimize the abuse, distance from you, and/or actively defend him, which only fuses her to him more; the "us against the world" phenomenon. This operates whether she is with him or not, but especially DO NOT FALL INTO THE TRAP OF TAKING SIDES WHEN SHE HAS LEFT HIM. She may say she hates his guts, he's the biggest jerk on the face of the earth, and she never wants to hear

[1] U.S. Department of Justice, Bureau of Justice Statistics, Press Release, Violence Against Women: Estimates from the Redesigned Survey, August 1995.

his name again. It's tempting to at least agree with her. Don't do it. No matter what she is saying now, SHE WILL LIKELY CHANGE HER MIND SEVERAL TIMES before finally moving beyond this relationship. If you so much as agree with her now you may be on her opposing side tomorrow. And keep in mind, MOST BATTERED WOMEN LEAVE AND RETURN TO THEIR BATTERERS SEVERAL TIMES BEFORE THEY MAKE A FINAL BREAK.

Even when women do leave their batterers for good, they are usually not, in their minds, 100 percent gone! For quite a while after leaving them, most battered women have positive thoughts about their batterers; wishing they could get back together, yearning for the good times, craving their partner's touch. If you talk badly about your friend's or relative's partner, even during this "deprogramming" time, she is likely to believe that you will think she's foolish for having any positive feelings for him ("I should hate him, but instead, I miss him terribly"). If she holds these feelings from you, so you won't think badly of her, greater distance between you will be the result.

It is not necessary to take sides against him in order to show your support of her. Indeed, SUPPORT COMES IN THE FORM OF GOOD LISTENING; giving her full attention when she seems to need it, not necessarily waiting until she asks for it.

4. RESPECT HER DECISIONS, DON'T JUDGE HER. It is helpful to respect her decisions. It is not helpful to judge her decisions as either good or bad. Indeed, try to look at decisions as neither universally right or wrong. Sure, you probably have your own strong feelings about the way she *should* do things or should feel, but who is to say *you* are right? If you have never lived with an abusive partner you

can't possibly understand the conflicting issues and feelings she is balancing. If you have been abused, your situation was probably different from hers in many ways. One thing is certain, you don't have as much information as she has about her situation.

It may be extremely difficult for you to respect and not judge her decisions if you have seen her acting irrationally or making seemingly irrational decisions. If you look more closely at the decisions she makes concerning herself and her relationship with her partner, however, you might find that she is making very rational decisions considering the erratic circumstances in which she is living.

The bottom line is, you don't have to agree with the decisions she makes, just respect her right to make them. IF YOU DON'T AGREE WITH A DECISION SHE HAS MADE, YOU CAN SAY NOTHING OR SIMPLY SAY THAT YOU DON'T AGREE WITH THAT DECISION.

Focus on what you see that she does well rather than what you see as her failures. Show her that you recognize her inherent worth by telling her what you like about her or what she means to you. Of course, be careful to say what you truly believe, as YOUR DISHONESTY WILL NOT BOLSTER HER SELF-ESTEEM OR YOUR ROLE AS ANCHOR. You can tell her, for example, that you have respect for her abilities to make good decisions ("I know you to be rather careful in making your decisions"). Or you can express confidence in the actions she has chosen to take ("I know of many things you've done, which have turned out very well").

5. HONOR HER FEELINGS. Women in our society are often taught not to have aggressive feelings such as anger or impatience. We are taught to avoid conflicts and help

everyone else feel happy. Because of this early life training, battered women (like most women) often have to struggle to acknowledge their own negative feelings, much less to express them appropriately. And since a battered woman's feelings are also squelched and negated by her batterer through the course of their relationship, she begins to numb herself so that she feels very little. The fear eventually becomes smaller and the pain duller over time. This detachment from their own feelings allows battered women to stay in relationships with men who can be very scary.

Most battered women, then, could benefit from an anchor who acknowledges *all* of her feelings as neither right nor wrong. They are, simply, hers. For you to criticize her feelings is to fail to recognize her humanity. You can help her recognize her own feelings by mirroring them for her (as discussed in Chapter Five) or by simply asking, "How do you feel about that?" I can't emphasize the usefulness of this simple question enough. Indeed, Jackie found this to be the single most helpful question in her new repertoire of questions. She was very uncomfortable asking it at first. It seemed too probing and personal. However, she was always surprised at her friends' or relatives' response; they invariably appreciated the concern and shared more of themselves in answer to that question than she ever expected.

Another way to express respect for her feelings is by showing her that you allow yourself to have uncomfortable feelings. You can do this by talking about your own feelings. For example, "I feel afraid for you when you tell me how your husband pushes you around." If she was feeling afraid of her husband when he pushed her around, knowing that you also feel afraid may help to validate her feeling.

If you are a woman, it might be especially helpful to appropriately share feelings which are considered by many not to be feminine, like anger or frustration. If you are a man, it might be helpful for you to talk about feelings you have which people don't commonly accept as being "manly," like sadness, anxiety, or fear. In these ways you can show her that you believe all feelings are acceptable.

In order for you to do what I am suggesting here, you must be aware of your own feelings and the differences between feelings and thoughts. I make this distinction because many people I have counseled tended to confuse the two. When I asked, "How did that make you feel?" They responded with a thought, "I didn't think it was very important." Examples of feelings are: sad, mad, happy, frustrated, nervous, excited, lonely, scared. PRACTICE THINKING ABOUT YOUR OWN FEELINGS AND YOU WILL BECOME BETTER ABLE TO EXPRESS THEM.

If you continue to have difficulty expressing your feelings appropriately you might enlist her aid in finding *you* help. Like anyone else, battered women need to feel needed. It would probably greatly help her self-esteem to be able to turn the tables and help you find help toward personal growth.

6. DON'T GIVE ADVICE. For you to offer advice or accept her invitation to give it has essentially the same effect as judging her feelings or decisions. It implies that her feelings are somehow wrong and that she can't make good decisions on her own. GIVING ADVICE TENDS TO TAKE AWAY HER POWER. Taking away her power is what her batterer does best. She doesn't need for you to do that.

Some abused women have never learned to trust their own feelings or instincts, nor do they view themselves as good decision makers. Other battered women felt confident in those areas before the abuse began, but the process of living in a battering relationship destroyed the confidence and replaced it with shame and self-doubt. A batterer will consistently send his partner messages that she is nothing without him; i.e., she makes bad decisions, everything she touches turns sour, no matter what she does she can't win, she's too fat or too lazy or too this or too that. He might also undermine her decisions in such a way as to make them come out badly, and then remind her regularly of what poor decisions she makes. Through his emotional abuse she eventually loses her belief that she is a worthwhile person who has normal feelings and can make good decisions.

I counseled a couple in which the husband had stopped his physical abuse of his wife upon entering counseling, only to keep her awake each weekday night to "discuss" their marital problems (although he did all the talking while she was expected to listen quietly). She was a bus driver and decided to quit her job since she was falling asleep at the wheel, due to exhaustion. He agreed that she should quit, at the time, but they subsequently struggled financially with the loss of income from her job. Her husband, then, used the incident to berate her, saying that she was lazy and made poor decisions. She began to agree with him, forgetting about the original reason she decided to quit, and felt more worthless and depressed than ever before.

Most battered women, at one point or another, suffer from a very poor self-concept. For you to give her advice is like saying to her, "I agree, you are pretty worthless! Look at the stupid decisions you make. But fortunately you have me, in my wisdom, to tell you how to feel and what to do."

That message is the opposite of what will help her regain the sense of power she needs to get back in touch with her feelings and to make decisions in her own best interest.

In addition to the above consideration, for her to follow your advice may put her in great danger. You are not responsible for her partner's violence whether or not she follows advice you give her. Nevertheless, you would probably feel awful if she did what you suggested only to end up beaten or dead. To stay away from giving advice means that you are taking control of your own behavior in a way that frees her to feel better about her own decisions. Furthermore, she's in a better position to make safer decisions if she is confident of her own abilities and feelings than if she lacks that belief in herself.

So what can you do instead of giving your advice? It is crucial that you encourage her instead to regain confidence in herself and her ability to make the choices that will be best for herself and her children. You can turn questions back to her: "What do you think you should do?" Then, you can support her answer: "You're the one who knows your situation best." And as stated previously, you can actively help her feel better about her own ability to make good decisions by reminding her of specific decisions she has made which have worked out well ("Remember when you decided to get tutoring for little Amy last year? She's really reading well now.").

7. CONTROL YOURSELF, NOT HER. Control is an issue that encompasses the previous two issues but can also take on other forms. It can be a subtle control: parents promising their daughter to put her through college if she stays away from her abusive partner. Or it can be direct control: a woman attempting to keep her friend from

going back to her batterer by telling her she won't talk to her anymore if she gets back together with him. Control can come from another direction completely: through in-laws threatening to cut off monetary support of their grandchildren should their daughter-in-law *not* return to their son.

There are infinite numbers of ways people try to exert control over other people. This is human nature to a degree and is not inherently bad. It becomes potentially hurtful when that control attempt is toward a mentally sound adult and is coercive, manipulative, threatens force, or uses force. You certainly cannot be an effective anchor if you continually attempt to control your friend or family member, whether subtly or directly. But to loosen your control within a relationship is much harder to accomplish than it would seem since most people are not consciously aware of the control methods they use to get their way. When you care about a battered woman you might find yourself wanting so desperately for her to stay away from her batterer, for her own safety, or the children's safety, that you may be surprised to see yourself using controlling methods you never knew you knew.

What's more confusing is that there is a difference between coercive or forceful control of someone and the type of control in which you assign consequences of your own to their behavior. The quality of the former is punitive and will work only to alienate her from you, "I'm going to teach you to do as I say." The quality of the latter is self-controlling/limit setting, "I will have to take this action for myself if you choose to take that action." When I worked in a battered women's shelter we had a rule that any woman resident of the shelter who told her abusive partner the location of the shelter would have to move out. I would tell women who broke this rule, "In your choice to disclose the location of our shelter you have put yourself and the rest of us in danger. Because of that, you will have to move out." They made the choice to break the rule. They would be the one to face the consequences of that decision. To exercise this kind of control, being clear about your own limitations within a relationship, is your right and responsibility.

Ask yourself, "How do I tend to control situations within relationships?" By observing yourself in relationships you can discover in which situations you tend to try to exert too much of the punitive type of control over others. If you practice thinking of things in terms of controlling yourself and not others, your feelings will begin to change and you will actually *become* less punitive and more self-aware.

8. SHOW HER YOUR REALITY. As I discussed earlier, living within the chaos inherent in the cycle of violence, battered women often lose their perspective about themselves, who they are, and how they've changed to accommodate their batterer. A battered woman is usually so manipulated by her partner into thinking the way he wants her to think that access to reality, as perceived by much of the outside world, is lost to her. To become more aware of who she used to be and who she still is inside can help a battered woman see how much of herself she is giving up to be with him. This awareness can then motivate her to take action to reclaim her lost self.

One way you can help toward that goal is to BE A HISTORIAN FOR HER. You can gently and without judgment or criticism remind her of how she used to be: "You used to have lots of friends and enjoyed hanging out at the gym" or "You used to take such good care of yourself. Lately, you don't seem to care." Try to be more an observer than an opinion or advice giver.

You can also help her see a reality different from the one her abusive partner has thrust upon her by noticing and commenting on inconsistencies or falsehoods which she seems to believe. For example, the woman you care about is the main breadwinner of the family but she tells you that her partner believes that she is lazy and she is wondering how true that is. You might choose to express your point of view; that it seems to you that a woman who holds a job which brings in the majority of the monetary support for the family can't possibly be lazy. Or, you might express confusion concerning the inconsistency. "I'm confused. You're telling me that you work enough to bring in most of the money for the family, yet you're also wondering if you're lazy?"

Another example: Yesterday, your abused friend told you that she has always dreamed of going back to college and that now she would like to try to do that. Today, she tells you that she and her partner are planning for her to open a day-care center in their home to bring in extra money. You can observe the inconsistency without judgment or criticism: "I'm confused. Yesterday you told me you wanted to go back to school and today you're saying you're starting to do day care." That's all you have to say. Let her explain the inconsistency. That will help her become aware of the confusing aspects of her life and what her true feelings and beliefs are.

One opinion that I think is usually very helpful to share with a woman who has been battered is, "YOU ARE NOT THE ONE AT FAULT FOR YOUR PARTNER'S ABUSE. HE IS!" You must, of course, first believe this yourself! If you do believe this, let her know that she can't be responsible for his behavior any more than you can be responsible for hers. Nothing she could possibly do deserves a violent or abusive response. He has choices of how to respond in any given situation. He can choose nonabusive ways of handling his feelings, just as millions of other men do in their intimate relationships.

9. TRY TO EMPATHIZE WITH HER WHILE MAINTAINING YOUR OBJECTIVITY. I had a client once who tried, several times, to go to her parents for help after her boyfriend hit her. They became so hysterical when she told them of his abusive behavior that she didn't tell them about subsequent abusive incidents because their reactions made her feel more overwhelmed and helpless than she already felt. This example illustrates why it is important that you attempt to achieve a delicate balance between your being emotionally available and maintaining enough objectivity so as not to be sucked up into the same roller coaster of feelings she is experiencing. This balance is what makes you a safe person to go to, what makes for a good anchor.

Being conscious of using other good communication skills will go a long way toward helping you maintain that difficult balance. And to do that you must try to remain calm, even if she is telling you something very disturbing. AN EFFECTIVE ANCHOR IS CALM; NOT UNAFFECTED, BUT CALM. This means that you will have uncomfortable feelings about what she is telling you. However, no matter how angry or afraid or worried you feel, you must control your reaction in front of her so that you show yourself to be self-controlled. As in the previous example, she won't trust you if she has to worry about you "freaking out."

If you notice that your body is starting to react to the stress (i.e., tightening of the throat, nauseated stomach, sweaty palms), go to a separate room for a few minutes and count to one hundred, or learn another way to relax when stressed. Jackie took breaks away from her anchor role for several weeks at a time when she became especially tired or overwhelmed. Of particular importance: if you have trouble expressing your own anger appropriately and non-violently, get professional help before attempting to become an anchor for someone.

Many women who are abused have times when their minds race, thoughts are jumbled together, and they talk a mile a minute. Particularly when she first comes to you for help, be prepared for your abused friend or relative to be in a hurricane of thoughts and feelings. She may be looking so far ahead and at such a huge number of problems and decisions facing her that she has trouble sorting them out. When you see her she may talk incessantly and jump from problem to problem, or story to story, without pause.

Often, battered women who are allowed to safely spill their stories will eventually slow that down themselves and maintain focus on one problem without you doing anything other than listening. However, if you notice that she has "spilled" with you several times and doesn't seem to be changing or slowing down, to continue that pattern could be unproductive for her and your relationship with her. You may need to make an attempt yourself to slow down the conversation so that she can think rationally about one problem at a time. You can do this by gently asking her to slow down her end of the conversation or asking her to focus on one topic ("Could you tell me more about the topic we were discussing a few minutes ago?"). The tough part for you is not to let *your* end of the conversation get sidetracked, even if she slips back into the storm. You may regularly have to refocus the conversation back to a particular topic. Do so gently and with as much tact as you can muster. It can be very frustrating talking with someone who is talking out of a hurricane. If you can maintain your focus on the subject at hand, regardless of what she does, that will be helpful in itself.

A tried and true way of keeping yourself focused is to ask how she currently feels or how she felt when she was in the situation she's describing. This tends to keep both you and her focused on what is really important—her experience—rather than endless details.

A related problem you might face is getting caught up in your own hurricane out of panic that if you don't say the right thing, quickly, you may never get another chance. You might find yourself frantically grasping for anything to say that will change her mind or will positively impact her out of fear that she will make the wrong decision and be hurt or killed if you don't make a big impact on her. This is usually a disguised rescue attempt and is easy to slip into.

When you notice yourself talking fast and forced with a sense of panic about you, watch out! When I feel this way (usually when I'm talking to a battered woman and I know I only have one chance of limited time to speak to her), it helps me to think longer-term, beyond the current conversation—what I am saying now is only planting a seed in hopes that it will grow. I might even tell myself to presume that the woman I am talking with will return this time to her abusive partner and my goal with this conversation is simply to help her feel comfortable enough talking with me about the abuse that she will realize I am there for her to talk to the next time he hurts her. By telling myself that, I set myself up to expect only what I have some control over, which is being with her in a way that promotes her trust of me.

10. BE A GOOD MODEL, FULFILL YOUR OWN NEEDS. You can't be an anchor for a person unless your own needs are being fulfilled, and anchors have plenty of needs! To be an anchor requires a large investment of time and emotional energy. Be aware of your own needs and take action to fulfill them. That may mean that you take a walk every day to have thinking time, call a friend in to be *your* anchor, or take time away. Remember, when Jackie was overwhelmed or just plain tired, she took a break of several weeks at a time during which she wouldn't initiate contact or even think about Diane's situation. Jackie usually spent a lot of time thinking about Diane, a very draining thing for her. During her weeks "off" she would do things she knew would give her back energy and keep her mind off Diane. She would accept calls from Diane, just not initiate them herself.

Although it is important to maintain regular contact with the abused woman you care about, you still need breaks. The important thing is that your break doesn't become permanent distance. Depending on the type of relationship you and your friend or relative have, you may feel comfortable telling her that you won't be calling her for a few weeks (give her a clearly delineated amount of time if you possibly can) because you will be spending some rejuvenation time by yourself. You don't need to give her your whole line of reasoning. You will be showing her that you have the right to take care of yourself just as she has that same right.

11. LET HER KNOW HOW YOU CAN AND CAN-
NOT HELP. If she feels comfortable enough with you she
might directly ask for your help. If she hasn't asked you for
help and it seems appropriate, you can ask her directly,
"How can I help?" Under either circumstance, be honest
with her about what you are willing and able to do—your
limits ("I can let you stay in my apartment for one month
but then you will have to find a different place because my
other roommate will be returning home"). If you are not
clear with her about your limits or if you help her in such a
way that you feel used up, you will resent her and neither
of you needs that. For example, if you agreed to let her
stay at your home upon escape from her abusive husband,
and you knew her husband would be looking for her there,
you would be doing yourself and her a disservice.

Only you can determine what your personal limits are.
If you are unable to help her in the way she is request-
ing, try not to let guilt cloud your judgment. You may, instead, be able to help her find someone else who can do
what she is asking. Remember, battered women's shelters
and outreach shelter services exist now in most areas of the
United States. She might want your help in finding the
number for the shelter group in your area, or the district
attorney's office, or the low-income housing office. Be
clear and honest with her whatever help you decide you
can give. Don't promise something you can't deliver. And
always be aware of your own safety requirements and
those of your family. (See Appendix I, "Advocacy," for
more ideas on how you can help.)

If the abused woman you care about has not asked you
directly for help and if it doesn't seem appropriate to ask
what she needs help with, you can make suggestions of
ways you might be of help to her. Perhaps you have some

extra money you can give her for groceries, but you know she would never ask you for money. You can offer to give it to her in a way that she could more easily accept it, as a birthday present, loan, etc. As always, though, honor what she says in final answer to you.

12. SUGGEST WAYS OF HELPING HER WHICH DON'T HAVE STRINGS ATTACHED (YOU DON'T EXPECT ANYTHING IN RETURN). One way to do this is to freely offer your help to her while she is with her partner. Perhaps you could baby-sit her children so she can have some time to herself. You might provide transportation to places she needs to go. I know of one woman, of modest means herself, who would help her daughter by buying toys for her children at garage sales, since the daughter's husband wouldn't allow his wife to buy toys with "his" money. Any help that is given free of your control or judgment will show her that your intentions are purely to care for her. Too often family members and friends are only helpful if their loved one leaves her abusive partner. This can leave the impression that they are trying to manipulate her into staying away from him.

One way your battered friend or relative might ask you to be of help is by giving her your counsel. For instance, she might ask you to analyze her situation—"Why do you think I keep going back to a man who beats me?" LET HER KNOW EARLY ON IF SHE COMES TO YOU FOR THIS TYPE OF HELP THAT YOU ARE NOT CAPABLE OF COUNSELING HER IN THESE MATTERS and that you recommend she seek professional counseling to help her with issues surrounding the abuse. There are many possible reasons for her to ask for your counsel. She might sense that she needs psychological help but not know how or where to get it. Or, if she is like many people, she may feel afraid to get professional counseling because of preconceived ideas about it. Regardless of what her reasons are, be gentle and consistent in refusing to play the counselor role for her. You can, perhaps, tell her that you will help her find a good counselor/therapist and maybe accompany her to the first visit if she wants that. You might also recommend literature on the subject of domestic violence which could provide her with enlightening information regarding her circumstances.

WHEN TO TAKE ACTION ON HER BEHALF AND WITHOUT HER DIRECTION

The principles discussed in this chapter are not hard-and-fast rules, they are general guidelines. Before employing any particular plan when relating to a woman in a dangerous and abusive relationship, you must consider the context of both her situation and your own.

There are times when it is not appropriate for you to wait until being asked before you take decisive action to help a battered woman. Those are usually situations in which she is in immediate danger and can't ask for help or do what needs to be done to ensure her own safety. For example, if you see your friend next door being pushed around by her husband in their backyard and she is upset, screaming for him to stop, you might decide it is safer to call the police and report it, than to not do anything. If your sister frantically calls you at 3 A.M. telling you her boyfriend has a gun and is shooting up the house, then she hangs up abruptly, you might decide to call the police and report it without waiting to discuss the matter with her first.

When the situation you are observing is difficult to judge, as domestic violence situations have the tendency to be, you must rely on your best knowledge and instincts. What would she want you to do under these circumstances? Have you discussed that with her? What is the usual police response to domestic violence cases in your area? Do they have policies designed to ensure the safety of the victim after they leave the scene?

Be aware that batterers usually get angry when police are called on them. And they do sometimes try to take it out on their partners (and, perhaps, the person who reported the incident to the police) when the police leave. To protect yourself, you can give your report anonymously. To protect her, the police should be trained on how to handle domestic violence calls to minimize the risk of him hurting her when they leave. For example, they should arrest the suspect if there is probable cause to do so. But, to be realistic, some police departments don't yet have pro-arrest policies and are still not trained very well in this area. Try to learn how your police department handles domestic violence calls *before* you are in the position of having to decide whether or not to depend on them.

In a crisis, if you are safely able to talk to your friend or relative about her immediate circumstances without putting her in more danger, then first ask for her impressions and what she thinks is best to do. In most situations, during the actual violent episode, you won't be able to safely discuss with her what to do. You will usually have to use your best judgment. When in doubt always err on the side of safety!

ANSWERS TO THE QUESTIONS YOU MIGHT HAVE

What should I do if the woman I'm concerned about asks me for my advice?

I suggest that you stay clear of the temptation to give her advice even when she asks you for it specifically. Indeed, many battered women feel very dependent on others to make their decisions for them, and they may be very convincing in their attempts to elicit advice. Regardless of why you give advice to the woman you care about, the results are the same; she will probably end up feeling less adequate to make good decisions in the future and less adequate with respect to her own feelings. And someone who *feels* less adequate usually *is* less adequate.

I let my friend stay with me after her husband beat her up. After a few days she started calling him to talk about their relationship. One day he showed up at my apartment! She had given him our address, even though I had asked her not to. I got really mad and kicked her out. What could I have done instead?

I can understand your anger. Probably without meaning to, your friend put you, and herself of course, in a potentially dangerous position. As I said in Chapter Two, battered women may not see the danger in their own situation and might inadvertently make decisions which put their friends or relatives in dangerous situations.

Without blaming or condemning her you still had to take action to provide for your own safety, even if she was not able or willing to do the same for herself. You could have said something like, "Since you let your husband know where you are, we are both in danger. I am not going to let myself be in that position and so I need for you to move to a different place. I will help you find another, safer place if you want me to." Her feelings may have been hurt, but that shouldn't have swayed your resolve to do what was safest. Remember, under the circumstances, it was also in her best interest to move. Moreover, for you to be cautious in that way might have emphasized to her that her own fear of her husband was legitimate.

CHAPTER SEVEN

About the Batterer

As a potential anchor to a woman who is being abused in her relationship, you will probably have some degree of contact with her abusive partner. But even if you don't, this chapter is designed to give you some information about batterers so that you know better the type of man you and your battered friend or relative are dealing with. What you don't know about batterers could hurt you!

WHAT DOES A BATTERER LOOK LIKE?

Do you think you could spot a man who batters his partner? You might believe that someone who does such awful things to a woman in private must look the part in some way. You might also think that an abusive man can't control his violent tendencies when he's under stress, even in public, and that he'll fly off the handle. You might not believe me when

I tell you that THE ODDS ARE THAT SOMEONE YOU KNOW IS BATTERING HIS PARTNER.

Batterers are not monsters. They don't even look violent to most people who know them. They don't walk around clenching their fists, ready to blow, their eyes shooting rays of hatred at whomever crosses their path. They are people, like you and me, and they look and act like us when they are among us. There are batterers who are financially prosperous and appear to have successful relationships. On the other side of the spectrum, there are those who are not able to sustain a job or significant personal relationships at all. Others fit somewhere in-between. Many batterers are especially charismatic, generous people, who have a passion for life and fun to which people are drawn. It is usually only when they are in intimate, committed relationships that they allow their unusual needs for security and control to surface, and then it is usually only shown to their victims.

There are some batterers who will display parts of their violent side to the people who know them. Employers, fellow employees, and friends may see signs of a batterer's abusive tendencies: emotional instability, lack of social skills, or general hostility. For example, at work he may have difficulty accepting others' authority over him or not work well with coworkers. He may seem to have a chip on his shoulder. He may frequently blame other people or things for problems he creates himself, and if he is conniving and manipulative, as many batterers are, he will present himself and his situation in such a skillful way that others often believe his excuses. His friends (if he has them) may hear him treat his partner disrespectfully or talk about her with irreverence. They may notice that he gets too mad too easily or that he's an "angry drunk." It is unlikely, how-

ever, that acquaintances and friends are witness to his actual acts of physical violence toward his partner. He uses
his formidable control skills to keep, not alienate, his own
allies; he manages his facade carefully to look like a pretty
good guy.

His family is often a different story. They probably
know him and his history well enough that he can't easily
fabricate a nice guy image with them. That does *not* mean
that they are likely to help his battered victim or you in
your efforts as anchor to her. They have problems of their
own, significant enough to produce a batterer. Many batterers grew up in families in which they were abused as
children or witnessed one parent abusing the other, so it is
unlikely that a batterer's family will come to the aid of his
partner when he continues the legacy of violence against
her. Instead of helping the batterer's victim, his family will
usually either vehemently defend him or distance themselves from the situation altogether because they have
given up trying to get him out of trouble. Only a few times
in my counseling practice with battered women did I see a
batterer's relative help his victim. In one situation the batterer's mother helped her daughter-in-law because she had
also been a victim of her husband's (the batterer's father)
abuse and therefore strongly identified with her daughter-
in-law. In another situation the batterer's sister helped her
sister-in-law because her brother was also abusive to her.

You, as a relative or friend of a batterer's victim, are the
most likely outsider to be witness to (or, less often, experience yourself) his abuse if you spend a lot of time around
the couple. He might belittle his partner or push her
around in front of you. He might even attempt to intimidate you directly using thinly veiled threats: "Mind your
own business, or someone you love is going to get hurt!"

He might actually want you to know he has violent potential so as to scare you away from being her anchor. That puts him in a more powerful position with her. Rarely, however, would he allow you to view his *most* violent behavior. He saves that for his partner, in private!

HOW DO YOU VERIFY A BATTERER?

Since batterers are not often easy to spot, how do you know if someone is a batterer? My answer to that is, YOU WILL ONLY KNOW FOR CERTAIN WHETHER OR NOT SOMEONE IS A BATTERER IF THE VICTIM OF HIS ABUSE CONFIDES IN YOU, IF THE BATTERER CONFESSES TO THAT FACT, OR IF YOU WITNESS HIS VIOLENCE FIRSTHAND. It won't help your position as anchor to condemn anyone to the status of batterer before you know the facts, so try to spend less time speculating about him and more time listening to the woman you care about. This is not to say that you should remain naive about batterers or their potential for violence. Knowing the characteristics common to most batterers puts you in a safer and potentially more helpful position. IN DOMESTIC VIOLENCE SITUATIONS, WHAT YOU DON'T KNOW CAN HURT YOU OR SOMEONE YOU LOVE.

DON'T FOCUS ON THE "WHYS"

A trap that you, as anchor, can easily fall into is spending valuable energy trying to understand why the abusive partner behaves the way he does, in hopes that you can somehow feel in control or even get him to give up his violent

ways. Indeed, his partner probably also hopes to understand him. Many battered women go to counseling and
read everything they can get their hands on about domestic violence in hopes they can *do something* so he will change
and their relationship will return to the rapture they had
before he became violent. What they find, if they look to
knowledgeable sources, is that they have the power to effect only their own change, and that their partner will continue to be violent unless he gets help himself (and even
then there are no guarantees that he will change with the
aid of counseling).

If you hope to understand a batterer so that you can
somehow make him change, forget it. It won't work. If you
try, on the other hand, to become more knowledgeable
about batterers in general, so that you can learn the safest
alternatives to choose in dealing with him or helping his
partner, you will be gaining real control over your life. You
as anchor, then, can help to empower the battered woman
you care about by being a living demonstration of the concept that REAL CONTROL OVER YOUR OWN LIFE IS
NOT ABOUT CONTROLLING ANYONE BUT YOU.

WHAT DOES SHE SEE IN HIM?

Contrary to what many people believe, most batterers
have some very attractive sides to them. They can be gentle, thoughtful, intelligent, nurturing with children—all the
things women usually look for in a partner. Furthermore,
those attributes are the only ones a batterer shows his partner for the first months or even years of their relationship.
Even when the abuse is in full swing, MOST BATTERERS
SPEND MUCH MORE TIME AS THE "GOOD GUY"
THAN AS THE "BAD GUY." Many battered women have

told me that they felt more appreciated and special with
their batterers than with any other man they have been
with. Their relationship with their batterer has the fire-
works women are taught to expect when it's true love.
Even when women get out of abusive relationships and
into healthy ones, they don't often experience the same
quality of ecstasy that they had with the abuser. So, in the
beginning, a woman falls in love with what appears to be a
wonderful man. They grow to depend on one another and
are blissfully happy together, for a while.

WHAT ARE BATTERERS REALLY LIKE?

When I first met Joe he spoke frequently of his love for animals. I love animals, too, so I thought he and I might have a
lot in common. He appeared also to be very concerned
about human rights, a champion of the less fortunate. This
impressed me because, as a budding social worker, I advo-
cated for the advancement of civil rights. I thought I'd
found a gentle and intelligent friend to share time with.

I didn't realize until much later that his gentleness was
really a passivity common to batterers (they have trouble
being assertive and let anger build up until it blows, like
the top off a pressure cooker). His concern for the rights of
others was really a projection of his own self-pity. He felt
very sorry for himself, thinking everybody was against
him. He believed others should care for him enough to excuse his irresponsible and abusive behavior.

Most of the time Joe displayed the caring, gentle, fun-
loving side I liked. But a few times over the course of
our three-year relationship he showed a monstrous side—
always when he feared I was leaving the relationship. Once,

when I told him I thought we needed to break up, he initially accepted it with reasonable sorrow ("I'm sorry this isn't working out but it probably is best"). Then rapidly, over the next few minutes, his whole demeanor changed. He worked himself into a rage that I could do nothing about. His eyes glazed over, he started grinding his teeth and pacing the floor. His whole body became taut, like a rope at its breaking point, and his voice rose. I thought, if I try to leave now, he'll turn his anger toward me. If I stay I might have to endure his crazed ranting for a while, but he'll probably calm down eventually, if I remain calm. So I decided to stay. Soon he was talking incessantly about what a screw-up he was and how I deserved better. After an hour or so of buildup he grabbed a chair and threw it against the wall, breaking it into three pieces. I was terrified, which was his intention. He wanted me to know that the chair could have been broken over my head, though he denied it at the time: "I was just so upset at the thought of losing you. I would never hurt you. You know that." Of course he did hurt me physically, about a year after this incident.

To a removed observer a batterer's violent rage might look like a two-year-old's tantrum, only in a much bigger, scarier body. To the person at whom he is directing his anger, however, a batterer seems like a monster when he is in his violent rage. His eyes are wild. He paces like a nervous cat, flails his arms about, yells, threatens, throws things, tears things up. Not to mention how he actually hurts his victim's body.

Many battered women I've known referred to their batterers as being like Jekyll and Hyde. The change from Jekyll to Hyde is so pronounced that women who have been battered describe a terrifying look that suddenly appears in a batterer's eyes which signals his changeover to violent monster. One minute he is the most loving and gentle man they have ever known, the next minute he is stalking her, ranting and raving, hitting and throwing.

To his victim, a batterer's behavior seems very irrational and out of the blue. His one side is so good, while the other is so bad. Confused, she wonders, "How can both of these sides be a part of the same man?" The monster seems so separate from the good guy that she believes there must be a way to eliminate it altogether. She might fantasize about being with him when he finally gets rid of the violent side. This belief might provide her with a lot of hope that things can and will change so that they can ultimately live together with only the happy times.

A battered woman might eventually begin to sense the buildup of tension which signals an impending blowup, but because it is in the batterer's best interest to remain unpredictable, he will inevitably do something unexpected to keep her guessing. His Jekyll-and-Hyde behavior serves to confuse her, keeping him in control and her off-balance yet still hooked into him.

HOW BATTERERS OPERATE

THE "TEST" PERIOD

No one falls in love with a monster. I believe that most batterers know this at some level and because they want love like anyone else, they can become very good at hiding their violent side. A batterer allows his partner glimpses of his violence very gradually and subtly. This is what I call the Test Period. During this period he may disclose that he was violent to a previous partner. He may throw objects at the wall or kick something. He may forcefully hold his partner's arms so that she will stay and listen to him while he rants and raves for hours about something as trivial as her failure to iron his blue jeans.

Though it might seem abundantly clear to *you* that his behavior during these tests is inappropriate, he will be able to explain that behavior to his partner so cunningly that she will probably dismiss these incidents as flukes. Her head may be whispering to her, "Leave him, he has done it again," but her heart is saying, "He didn't mean to hurt me. He's really a sweetheart inside." And her heart will usually win out over her head, especially if she was socialized to ignore her own instincts and judgments for the sake of making intimate relationships work. If she stays with her partner through his tests and even rationalizes them away, then he will probably feel safe to be even more abusive in the future.

Joe tested me several times over the course of our three-year relationship. Once, he casually mentioned that he had spent some time in a mental hospital. He explained that away by saying that his parents had him committed because they were uncaring people who didn't understand him. I believed him and, in doing so, passed his test!

Another time he admitted to having hit his ex-wife when they were together, giving her a bruised eye. Somehow, he managed to describe the incident in such a way that it seemed to me to have been an isolated event. I, in effect, excused it by accepting his minimized version of the story, thereby passing one of Joe's most significant tests with flying colors. In another test he hit a wall with his fist.

He gradually escalated the amount of violence in his tests of me until finally revealing his most terrifying side. That was the day, after I had broken up with him, that he held me captive and beat and terrorized me for eight hours. I don't accept any blame for what Joe did to me, but I learned a lot from that experience. I can see now that Joe's blowup was the culmination of several things, including that I was such a good test subject. He thought he had nothing to lose, that I would stick by him. I hadn't left after the tests before, he figured, why would I do so now? Maybe if he scared me enough I'd be too afraid not to come back to him.

Joe believed, at some level, that he could *make me* love him; a distorted logic common to most batterers. It seems like a ridiculous way of getting affection to most of us, yet to frighten and intimidate people works for batterers. They usually get their way, even if they don't get *real* love.

A BATTERER'S CONTROL

As individual as batterers are, a part of them is strikingly similar to other batterers. I call that the monster part. Two qualities within the monster part of a batterer are the most important for you, a friend or relative, to be aware of.

First, BATTERERS DON'T ACCEPT RESPONSIBILITY FOR THEIR MISBEHAVIOR. Many batterers don't consciously view what they do as wrong. They can be very good at justifying their own treatment of their partners ("I had to hit her, she wouldn't quit nagging at me"), even while they are criticizing the abusive behavior of another batterer ("That's awful the way that guy treats her").

An example of how justification works: a man who had physically abused his wife for many years once told me that he had to beat her occasionally in order to teach her a lesson because she was lazy and put off cleaning the house when she was working long hours at her job. He thought his intentions were basically good. He saw it as his right and duty, for the benefit of the family, to "teach" his wife right from wrong using his fists.

Most batterers have never learned to be accountable for their actions, but they have learned well how to shift blame for their misdeeds onto others. To outsiders who don't know his history very well, a batterer might appear to have really bad luck. He always seems to work for the unreasonable boss, his landlords expect too much, his teachers pick on him, or his parents don't ever do anything for him, despite his relentless efforts to try to get along with all these people. His battered partner may also believe his rendition of these stories, until she starts to see his pattern of martyrdom or when she becomes the one who is blamed.

Second, BATTERERS HAVE AN INSATIABLE NEED TO CONTROL THOSE PEOPLE WHO ARE IMPORTANT TO THEM. Underneath any batterer's facade lies an insecure child who is terrified of being abandoned or hurt. Many batterers grew up in violent homes in which they were abused or neglected by their parent(s) or one parent abused the other. Somewhere in his development he learned to control people so that he didn't have to experience those uncomfortable feelings from childhood. He also learned that VIOLENCE AND ABUSE WORK TO GET HIM THAT SENSE OF CONTROL HE CRAVES.

A batterer's specific method for control at any given time will depend on the particular circumstance or what method works for him. He uses forms of emotional control in the early stages of an intimate relationship, and continues to use them after the physical abuse begins.

It may seem to you that batterers behave abusively

because they *can't* control themselves. Indeed, many batterers I've known believed the same thing, that they completely lost control of themselves when they got angry. I believe that most batterers are under their own control, though it may be at a subconscious level.

Evidence that batterers do exercise some control over their violent behavior: (1) A batterer is much more likely to kill his partner when he has reason to believe that she has left him for good and there is no chance of winning her back, than when she is with him. (2) Batterers are careful to strike their victims in such places on their bodies that marks or bruises won't be seen by outsiders (or, in some cases, that they *will* be seen so that their victims will be too embarrassed to go to work, see friends, etc.).

If a batterer actually lost all control of his violent behavior he would not be able to stop himself before killing his partner during any acute battering incident. If a batterer is so filled with rage that he doesn't, at some subconscious level, know what he is doing, he wouldn't be able to determine where to place a punch so that evidence of his abuse doesn't show.

A batterer may appear to be very remorseful for having hurt his partner. He may actually *be* sorry for what he did. That doesn't mean that he is willing to stop himself from doing the same thing again. In most cases batterers do what benefits them. Concern for themselves and their own well-being outweighs any regard for others; however, they may be extremely adept at hiding that fact.

I've known of many batterers who were not only sorry but able to convince themselves that they could somehow (and usually without outside help) will themselves to eliminate their violent sides and be left with only their good sides. Suffice it to say, effective treatment for a batterer is much more complicated and time-consuming than simply exercising willpower (for more on treatment for batterers see Appendix II, "To Find Good Professional Help").

Most important, A BATTERER OFTEN BELIEVES HE WILL NOT BEAT HIS PARTNER AGAIN; therefore, he can look very sincere and be especially convincing to his partner and you when he promises never to hurt her again. His self-deception combined with the battered woman's own belief that he can eliminate his violent side, may draw her back to him with the strong conviction that *this time* he will change. Be careful that you are not also deceived.

EMOTIONAL CONTROL TACTICS

It is important that you be aware of the insidious and subtle nature of a batterer's emotional control of his partner and perhaps you, so that you can counteract the effects of those forces.

Using various forms of emotional control, a batterer can gradually brainwash his partner in such a way that she begins to doubt her own abilities, including the ability to change her situation. Furthermore, if his control tactics confuse her sufficiently, she won't be able to think clearly enough to even decide to leave, much less make a viable, safe plan to leave. Having stripped her confidence from her, he is free to treat her any way he wants, without fear of losing her.

Extreme jealousy is the hallmark of virtually every batterer. A batterer is often so insecure that he obsesses about his partner's activities, ruminates about where she is, what she is doing, and with whom. He grows more suspicious with the passage of time until deciding he must control her freedom of movement so as to keep her from abandoning him (which he may refer to as her "screwing around").

An example of how extreme a batterer's jealousy can become: one of my clients wasn't allowed to leave the house without her husband for fear that she would fall in love with another man the first time she was alone with one. He grew to accept her coming to counseling for help *for herself* only because I wasn't a man. Another client's husband didn't allow her to go grocery shopping because he had conjured up the idea that she was having an affair with the produce man. He did all the shopping.

Men who batter often attempt to control people by manipulating them into believing what they want them to believe. I've seen a batterer manipulate the facts of his case so skillfully that the judge was convinced he didn't beat his wife, even though she came to court with black-and-blue eyes and police records corroborating her story.

The more intelligent a batterer is, the more adept he can be at getting his way using manipulative means, without anyone realizing what is really happening. He will probably be very convincing, even to the most careful observer. You may go into a conversation with a batterer thinking clearly and logically, yet end it feeling utterly confused and ignorant. You may start a discussion with him despising him and what he has done to your friend or family member but end it feeling sorry for him and even guilty that you ever thought badly of him. A batterer knows how to direct a conversation so that you feel like the one who has done something wrong.

Men who batter are often willing to intimidate those people they wish to control if manipulation isn't working to get them their way and if their obsessiveness over their partners is growing worse. There are many different ways they make others afraid of them without necessarily lifting a finger. Some batterers simply use direct threats of harm. Others imply that they will hurt the person whom they wish to control.

Still other batterers intimidate even more subtly, perhaps telling stories of the many fights they have won or how they were trained for special forces military combat. If you are the recipient of a subtle threat you may not even realize you're being intimidated. Indeed, you will probably feel it more as a vague uneasiness rather than fear. Regardless of which method(s) they use, the message batterers are sending through their statement of intimidation is the same: they are dangerous if they don't get what they want.

Another way batterers exercise control over others is by behaving very irrationally at times. Particularly when they are having a violent episode, their thoughts might be very illogical and fragmented. For example, "I thought I told you to clean up the yard before I came home. I hate the way you do the yard. My boss blames me for everything." Notice how the second thought contradicts the first, and the third thought doesn't have anything to do with the first two. It controls because it confuses.

Even though they can seem like it at times, most batterers are not mentally ill. According to Murray Straus, a leading domestic violence researcher, fewer that 10 percent of all instances of family violence are caused by mental illness or psychiatric disorders.[1] This can be disconcerting to both the battered woman and you who would like a logical explanation for his behavior and hope

[1]M. Straus, "A Sociological Perspective on the Causes of Family Violence," in *Violence and the Family*, edited by M. R. Green (Boulder, Colo.: Westview, 1980), pp. 7–31.

that, with traditional psychological treatment and maybe medication he will get "well."

A high percentage of batterers abuse drugs and/or alcohol. So do many battered women (see Appendix IV, "When the Woman You Care About Abuses Alcohol or Drugs"). The conventional wisdom in the domestic violence counseling field is that substance abuse and domestic violence are two highly correlated but separate problems. Many commonly abused substances (alcohol and other "street" drugs) make a person's violent behavior more severe than it would be without the substance, but they probably don't cause an otherwise nonviolent person to become violent. Many people have problems with drugs or alcohol but not all of them use violence.

Many battered women I've worked with hoped beyond hope that once their partners stopped drinking or drugging, they would stop beating them. That hope might even be enough to keep the women hooked into their relationships. Several of my clients even had the experience of their abusive partners entering substance abuse treatment. Among those partners who completed treatment there was a brief period of calm within the relationship after they came home. Eventually, however, my clients' partners began hurting them again although in some cases the abuse took on a different form, becoming more emotionally abusive than physically abusive.

A batterer consistently uses a combination of control tactics to evoke the desired response. What usually provides the strongest link in the chain of control and ties her to him with unimaginable power is physical control.

PHYSICAL CONTROL TACTICS

A batterer's physical abuse is the culmination of his ever-expanding needs for control and eventually becomes the main method for control. Think about how well it works. If you believed (because that person had been violent before) that you would be hurt or killed, or someone you loved would be hurt or killed if you didn't do what the threatening person wanted you to do, wouldn't you do it? You probably would, especially if you had been emotionally abused by that same person for months or years before the physical abuse began and you were feeling confused or helpless. COMBINE PHYSICAL CONTROL WITH EMOTIONAL CONTROL AND YOU HAVE A CONTROL SYSTEM THAT IS EXTREMELY DIFFICULT TO ESCAPE.

What forms of physical control are used by batterers? Raping, hitting, pushing, throwing, holding, squeezing, shooting, cutting, burning, kicking, scratching, slapping, suffocating, and as many other forms of torture as there are abusive thoughts.

SUMMARY

Most batterers look and act like ordinary people most of the time. They are usually especially careful to act like ordinary people in public or around people they are not familiar with. A batterer is an individual and, as such, has individual strengths and weaknesses, like all of us do. One batterer may be charismatic, charitable, and professionally successful while another might be irresponsible, asocial, or criminal. Most batterers are not mentally ill although some are.

You, as an outsider, are not likely to see a batterer's violent or abusive behavior directly, so you may believe that it doesn't exist or isn't as bad as his partner is expressing.

You can't judge a batterer by his facade. To do so might mean that you are denying, minimizing, or completely negating the battered woman's reality, while at the same time possibly supporting her hope that his abuse is not really as bad as it seems and will get magically better with enough time.

CHAPTER EIGHT

Safety

The way you handle your relationship with a man who has abused your friend or relative may be crucial to your own emotional and physical safety. An anchor must use very different skills in dealing with a batterer than those for relating to a battered woman, and though they are two distinct sets of skills, they are consistent with each other. With a batterer, as with a battered woman, you will still be acting like an anchor. With the batterer, however, you will need to be assertive and cautious.

As an added advantage of acting as an anchor when you're around a batterer, your role as anchor with his victim will be enhanced. She will see you being consistent in your behavior and this can promote her trust in you. She might also discover, through observing your behavior, how to emotionally and physically protect herself from her partner.

YOUR SAFETY

THE FRIGHTENING REALITY IS THAT BATTERERS SOMETIMES HURT OR KILL THOSE PEOPLE WHO ARE CLOSE TO THEIR VICTIMS. So, as a relative or friend of a battered woman, and particularly as an anchor for her, your life may be in danger, just as hers is. It is all too easy, however, to focus solely on her safety to the neglect of your own. You might feel somewhat insulated from the batterer's violence if he has never threatened you before. You might think that he wouldn't hurt you because he has no reason, you've done nothing to him. Unfortunately, things don't always work out that way.

By acting as anchor for his victim you empower her in such a way that she may decide to crawl out from under his controlling thumb. In a batterer's obsessive and controlling way of thinking, he may view this as a threat to his "love" relationship, indeed, a threat to his very existence. Just seeing you with her may represent to him his inability to control her every move or decision.

A batterer may first try to silence your influence on his partner by threatening, blackmailing, intimidating, or manipulating her regarding her relationship with you. One scare tactic he might use, for instance, is to tell his partner that, should she leave him, he will hurt someone in her family. If she is like most battered women, she will take this kind of threat very seriously because she knows that he can find her relatives and is capable of hurting them. Indeed, this kind of threat can be so powerful that it alone might work to scare her into submission.

If his attempts at control don't work to his satisfaction, however, he will probably resort to the more aggressive tactics which have worked for him in the past. And if he begins to view you as a source of power for her, as some-one standing between him and his relationship with her, he may turn his violence on you.

SARA'S ORDEAL

Remember my anchor Sara from Chapter Four? She was my good friend and roommate at the time Joe beat me up. After that incident, I moved out of the apartment Sara and I had shared, and in with my brother temporarily. I knew Joe would probably resort to threats or violence when his pleas for me to come back didn't work, and I didn't think he would find me at my brother's house. What I didn't count on was what he would do to Sara, who was still living at our apartment.

Joe went to the apartment one day and waited for Sara in the parking lot. When she came out to go to her car, he appeared, begging and intimidating her to get information about where I was. She denied his requests and kept walking to her car. He grew more and more enraged as each of his tactics failed. By the time Sara got in her car, Joe was furious. As she started the car and pulled away he began pounding his fists on the car window. He ran alongside the car, beating at the window until one hit broke through the glass. Terrified, Sara kept driving, running over the broken glass as she sped around the parking lot, trying desperately to get away. She managed, thankfully, to escape, even though the glass had flattened two of her tires. After this frightening ordeal, Sara knew she had to move out of the apartment and away from me permanently for the sake of her own safety. I understood her decision completely but did feel extremely responsible that my choice of a boyfriend caused her to have such an awful experience.

BE PREPARED

If you are attempting to become an anchor for a woman, it is safest to assume that her batterer is a danger to you. It is safer to prepare for the worst of what he is capable of and hope it never happens, than to hope it doesn't happen and be unprepared. I tell the same thing to battered women. SAFETY FIRST! That may seem elementary, but you'd be surprised at how easy it is to forget in the confusion of domestic violence situations. If you believe that a batterer could never do anything to hurt you, watch out! That is a dangerous belief to bet your life on. It can't hurt you to overreact and put yourself in as safe a position as possible, but it can hurt you to fail to do so.

HER SAFETY

You can't *make* your battered friend or relative choose the safest course of action for herself. What you can do is focus on safety yourself, as being the most important consideration in the midst of the chaos, not letting yourself become distracted from that focus by the multitude of complicated issues which present themselves along the way.

It is easy to get distracted because violent relationships often have a lot of peripheral turmoil going on. This happened to Jackie recently when she was presented with information about a friend's abuse. She became so preoccupied with the details of the abusive incident (who hit who, when, and how hard) that she forgot to consider the incident as dangerous to the woman she cared about.

For you to take your own safety seriously enough to take proactive measures may give the battered woman you care about a strong message that she can and should do the same for herself.

Jackie's Phone Call

To most abused women and potential anchors the risk of physical harm in domestic violence situations is much more easily seen and prepared for than the risk of emotional harm. Jackie, for one, was not prepared for her own emotional responses to a phone call she received one day.

When Jackie first heard Diane's stories about the emotional control tactics her husband used with her, she had a hard time understanding how it could work. In Jackie's words, "How can someone *make* you stay awake so that you will listen to them, or make you drink beer with them?" As her understanding of batterer control tactics and her listening skills improved, she began to be able to distinguish the brainwashed Diane (who sounded eerily like Diane's abusive husband, Mike) from the Diane she knew. One day, her own experience with Mike produced an understanding which helped answer her own questions. Jackie's story, in her own words:

> One time, Diane and her five-year-old daughter, Beth, visited our hometown to accompany a friend to the hospital. Diane had specifically told Mike she could not be reached while she was away and would call him later. When the phone rang at our parents' house and it was Mike, I was caught off guard. I answered the phone and made some small talk about Mike's new job, the one that was going to solve all their problems. He began to talk about missing Beth, and asked to talk to her. I thought this was a strange request because it was common

knowledge that he never showed affection toward her. Feeling a little uneasy and skeptical but willing to oblige, I put down the phone and went to the other room where she was playing. As soon as I told her that her father was on the phone and wanted to talk to her, Beth started crying and refused to go to the phone. The more I tried to coax her the more hysterical she became. My heart began to pound and the muscles across my shoulder blades tightened. What was I supposed to say to Mike? Beth's crying was so loud that I knew Mike could hear it. I proceeded to cover up the truth (that she refused to come to the phone), and told him that she was outside playing and had hurt herself. It was during this lie that my brain began to "shut down"; a feeling of overload, of being helpless in his clutches. I was looking for the right thing to do and yet nothing came. He was persistent in his request to talk to her, so in an attempt to get off the phone I cheerfully offered to summon her again. It was no use, she couldn't stop crying and wasn't about to talk on the phone. I dreaded going back to the phone and just wanted the conversation to end. I told him we could not get her to stop crying and maybe he should call later. He reluctantly agreed and the conversation was finally over.

When I had time to reflect on this situation later, I was concerned by my own reaction. I had been nervous and Beth frightened all because of a phone call made by an abusive man in another state. I could not remember the last time I told an out-and-out lie so someone else could save face. Why was I trying to protect him? Why did I try to cover up the truth? Why was I so nervous? Most disturbing was the fact that Mike had been able to control me from across the country using my own anxiety! Some understanding of my concerns came when I discussed them with Susan. . . .

First, I somehow felt responsible for "getting" Beth to come to the phone, even though she was terrified of her father and refusing to do so. She was terrified because of his abusive behavior, not mine, but he managed to handle our conversation in such a way that I ended up feeling responsible for her refusal, and even sorry for him!

Second, I was being manipulated by Mike. He timed the phone call when he knew we weren't expecting it; therefore, I was unprepared for how best to react. Furthermore, the more insistent he was to talk to Beth, the more nervous I became. When someone is persistent and demanding, my first tendency is to be polite and appeasing, not honest and assertive. I was raised that way.

Third, Mike needed to control Diane and Beth, but had to do so through me when I answered the phone, since Diane wasn't there and Beth was refusing to talk to him. I became the vehicle through which he was attempting to gain control of his wife and daughter.

Fourth, I wanted to make the situation with Beth look good so that Diane wouldn't have to endure a grilling by Mike about it when she returned home. Diane had told me that Mike would interrogate her about how things went and what was said for a whole week after she returned home from a trip away from him.

Fifth, I felt intimidated. I was worried about being found out by Mike. Mike had, prior to this incident, thought of me as his only ally in our family. I was afraid that if I was assertive with him, and told him the truth about Beth not wanting to come to the phone, he would see me as a foe and do something to inhibit my developing relationship with Diane. He had continually tried to turn her against the rest of our family, with a certain amount of success. I had become Diane's only real connection, and he would probably try to turn her against me, too, if he saw me as a threat to his control over her or Beth. Diane later told me that upon her return from her trip Mike mentioned to her that he couldn't believe my behavior on the phone. He said he would have expected that sort of suspicious behavior from anyone else in the family but not from me. I hadn't fooled him at all.

This experience helped me understand firsthand what my sister frequently went through in her marriage; feeling compelled to cover up disturbing truths and feeling mentally and emotionally "shut-down." Being caught off guard on a regular basis would make it difficult for anyone to sort through what was happening to them. Being afraid for your life on top of that, must be completely mind-boggling.

PRINCIPLES FOR PROACTION AND REACTION

In this section I discuss how you can act like an anchor so that you can effectively handle a batterer's attempts to control you emotionally and physically. The two situations are intertwined and, as I have been emphasizing in this chapter, you should always be aware of a batterer's potential for violence any time you deal with him. Remember, if he doesn't get his way with you one way he may try another, more dramatic, way. Educate yourself about and utilize the *safest* alternative to any situation involving a batterer.

These principles are intended to be of general help if you find yourself involved, in any capacity, with a man who batters. However, if you are in a position of immediate threat by him, they cannot necessarily be applied. For instance, if a batterer is holding you against your will and is hurting you or threatening to hurt you, you must follow your own instincts and judgment as to what is the safest course of action.

1. In dealing with an abusive individual you must TRUST YOUR INSTINCTS in recognizing when he might be trying to manipulate you. Being manipulated is similar to the feeling you get when a nice salesperson is trying to sell you something you don't want. Most people, when manipulated, get an uncomfortable feeling somewhere in their body. That feeling is trying to alert you to the fact that someone is intruding upon you.

It would have helped Jackie immensely in her conversation with Mike if she had just paid attention to her initial discomfort when the phone rang. Had she recognized that her feelings of discomfort were legitimate, instead of waving them aside, she might have handled the rest of the conversation with more assertiveness and regard for her own needs.

If a batterer wants to control you during a conversation, he might first try to confuse you. One way he might do this is by speeding up the conversation and by speaking in an aggressive, demanding tone, putting you on the defensive so that you say what he has set you up to say rather than what you *want* to say.

When you have an uncomfortable feeling in your body during a conversation with a batterer it can be helpful to just slow down. That may mean putting a stop to your conversation or changing its focus. You have the right to take time to regroup your thoughts. Try writing down ideas and feelings as soon as you can after you have them. This can help to make what is really happening clearer and more objective.

Even if Jackie had forgotten to pay attention to her early discomfort when the phone rang, she might have become aware of those uncomfortable feelings later in the conversation. It's never too late to pay attention to your feelings. She could have, at that point, stopped the conversation with or without an explanation. She didn't owe Mike an explanation. She could have said something like, "I need to go now, I can call you back later." That would have given her time to sort out her feelings. If he had protested, she could have simply repeated what she just said, as many times as she chose. She might have decided, if repetition wasn't working, to tell him she was going to hang up and do so. That was within her rights!

I believe that we human beings, like most animals, have something within us that tells us when we are in danger. In our society women, particularly, are encouraged to push those instincts for danger aside when to act upon them might make others uncomfortable or upset. This puts women at a real disadvantage when it comes to doing what is safest when they find themselves threatened by a batterer. Instead of listening to that instinctive voice inside telling them, "Get out of here or you're going to get hurt," they ignore it and reason with themselves, "I want to leave, but people are going to wonder about me if I leave right now. I had better stay and pretend that nothing is the matter."

Your instincts can help to protect you from harm, if you listen to and act upon them. My instinct for danger is a nauseous feeling in the pit of my stomach. I had to learn to pay attention to it, even though it didn't always seem logical or "polite" to do so.

You, too, can learn to be more aware of your own instinct signals so that you can act upon them when in danger. Remember that a batterer's threats may be very subtle.

If something inside you is telling you to get away from him, do it, even if it seems like an overreaction. Be aware that he might use your need to be "fair" or "friendly" to him to his advantage. You may choose to say something to him like, "What you're saying is scaring me. I'm leaving." Or, if it seems safer, just leave with no explanation. You don't owe him an explanation.

2. GOOD ANCHORS NEED ANCHORS THEM-SELVES is a principle that is just as important to use when dealing with a batterer as when you are trying to help a battered woman. Sharing feelings with someone you trust can be a crucial element in staying clear of manipulation. Jackie shared her feelings with me soon after she got off the phone with Mike. She felt very uneasy about her experience and knew she needed help sorting it out.

3. BE CAREFUL NOT TO COLLUDE WITH A BAT-TERER IN HIS ATTEMPTS TO MINIMIZE HIS VIO-LENCE OR SHIFT THE BLAME FOR HIS BEHAVIOR. In other words, if a batterer you know is minimizing or blaming someone else for something he did or is responsible for, don't react in such a way that you appear to excuse him or agree with him.

As I discussed earlier, batterers have particular difficulty assuming responsibility for their actions (a main reason it is so hard for them to change). They can be extremely skilled at making their abusive actions seem less dangerous than they are and at placing the blame for their problems on others. A glaring example of the latter: a batterer I coun-seled once told me in therapy that his wife deserved to get beaten by him that day because she didn't cook his egg hard enough though he had previously warned her several times to do so. In his mind, she had it coming. The woman in this example *was* responsible for not cooking his egg as hard as he liked, but she *was in no way* responsible for his violent reaction—he was. A batterer can be so convincing that you, too, may end up believing, as he does, that he wouldn't be having such a hard time if *those* people would just be nicer to him.

Even if you don't believe his excuses, it can be very easy to become a passive participant in a conversation with a batterer, inadvertently appearing to relieve him of his responsibility. A batterer is skilled at setting up conversations so that you will nod your head in agreement or say nothing at all. He is not likely to use open-ended questions or in any way invite you to disagree with him. Because he may make it difficult, in this way, to oppose what he is saying, you may need to take the lead and make a clear statement; that you believe he alone is responsible for his behavior and that that behavior is abusive or dangerous.

In the same vein, KEEP YOURSELF FROM TAKING RESPONSIBILITY IN ANY WAY FOR THE BATTERER'S BEHAVIOR. Since batterers can be so skilled at shifting blame for their self-imposed problems onto others, be careful not to allow him to make *you* feel guilty for something you didn't do.

What do you do if a batterer you know calls and sobs that you're standing in the way of his relationship with his kids since his wife and children fled for their lives after a beating, and you are concealing their location? You can remember that you weren't the one who did the beating; he was.

What if he calls you and says that his wife made him lose his job because her leaving caused him such anguish that he had to quit? You can remember that he was the one who quit his job, not his wife, and he is trying to shift blame away from himself. If you consistently let him know that you hold him responsible for his behavior, he'll most likely stop calling you and will find someone else who will excuse him.

4. USE ASSERTIVE LANGUAGE to address an abuser, particularly if he is trying to intimidate you. For example, if a batterer implies that he is going to hurt you, you can call it what it is. "That sounds like a threat to me. Are you trying to threaten me?" If he directly threatens you, you can also "name" the threat and tell him what you plan to do about it, "You are trying to threaten me and I will not talk to you anymore if you do that."

Among the couples I saw together in counseling, when some of the batterers made threatening gestures toward their partners, I always commented on it. "The look on your face is pretty scary. Are you trying to scare your wife?" He would invariably apologize or deny that he did it or meant any threat by it.

You may, of course, choose not to address him at all. If you do, as with his more subtle manipulations, do not play his game. He is much more practiced than you. A batterer doesn't understand direct, assertive ways of handling confrontations because he is used to people manipulating, threatening, and hurting each other when they don't agree. What throws a batterer off-balance quicker than anything is for you to be direct and assertive, not aggressive.

One client of mine who had battered his wife called me soon after his wife and children left him to go to a women's shelter. He said calmly to me, "Therapists get hurt sometimes when they don't do what their clients want." He was mad because I wouldn't tell him in which shelter his wife and children were staying. Though he didn't threaten my life directly, what he said gave me a very uncomfortable feeling in my stomach. I trusted that feeling and called his attention to his veiled threat. He backed way off, denying profusely that he intended to threaten me. Most tellingly, he never tried to threaten me again.

If you need further training in the area of assertiveness there are many good assertiveness training manuals which can help.

YOU CAN CHOOSE NOT TO TALK TO HIM AT ALL, OR TO NOT TALK WITH HIM UNTIL HE CALMS DOWN AND STOPS THREATENING YOU. You can inform him of your choice or just act upon it. You can choose not to answer the phone or door if you suspect it is him, hang up the phone if it is him, have your phone number changed, change homes, get an answering machine, or otherwise find a place to be where he isn't likely to find you.

Understand that unless you are very skilled and assertive, the more you agree to talk with him the more likely it is that you will find yourself being manipulated or threatened. Battered women grow to understand this tenet quickly and often decide not to talk with their batterer at all.

Many battered women I have worked with refused to talk to their batterer upon leaving him, even by phone from a safe place—that is, if they intended to stay away from him. They did this because they knew from experience that if they so much as talked to him over the phone he would somehow convince them to come back. The batterer will tell her how much he needs and loves her, that he doesn't understand why he hurts her but will never do it again. He will say how much the kids need their dad around and how important family is. He might imply that she is lost without him and that she can't make it without his income. He will remind her of the good times and promise that there are only good times ahead if she returns. BATTERED WOMEN KNOW FROM EXPERIENCE THAT IF THEY TALK TO THEIR BATTERER, THEY WILL PROBABLY RETURN TO HIM.

Six months after Diane left her husband to go live in the same city as the rest of her family, she agreed to talk with him for the first time since having left. In a matter of a few short minutes of conversation, she went from hating his lies and abuse to questioning whether she had conjured it all up in her mind. In those few minutes, over that long-distance phone call, he had begun to convince her that what she knew as her experience was totally false. Fortunately, Diane stayed in touch with her feelings and instincts after the call was over, and began talking to Jackie about it. Doing so helped her find her way to what she knew as the truth.

5. DON'T USE VIOLENCE OR THREATS OF VIOLENCE (or any of his control tactics for that matter) as an attempt to deal with a batterer. I reiterate, a batterer is most comfortable when someone counters his attempts at control using the same types of control methods. If you play his game, which he's already proven to be good at, he'll usually win. For you, only bad can come of it. A type of running feud can start in which each person tries to out-scare the other and so on and so on, until it escalates to the point where someone is killed. I'm talking here about using violence or threats of violence to punish the batterer or teach him a lesson—"If you hurt my sister again I'll kill you." Threats of this sort never stop batterers from being violent again.

Self-defense is a different story. Using violence or the promise of violent consequences to defend yourself or those you love may be necessary at some point when dealing with a batterer. However, there is a different emphasis when you use violence for self-defense than when you use it for punishment. Instead of trying to change a batterer's behavior with threats or violence, you can let the batterer know the immediate consequences to his actions, what you will do if he chooses to attempt to hurt you. Emphasize prevention and your willingness to follow through with consequences you promised. Self-defense laws differ from state to state, so find out what they are where you live, particularly if you plan on using a weapon for the sake of self-defense. And I strongly encourage you to use every available resource you can *before* violence (law enforcement and courts), to protect yourself and your family.

Some women I've worked with believed that if they could just hurt their batterer like he hurt them, he would feel what it was like and finally understand that he shouldn't do it anymore. So they fought back. A few women I've counseled had a little different twist to that, believing that a woman just shouldn't let her partner get away with hurting her. If she didn't, at least, defend herself by hurting him as badly as she was hurt, she was a wimp and deserved to be beaten. Those clients were very surprised when they tried to fight back with their abusive partners and the violence only escalated.

In my experience with couples in which the woman physically defends herself as a matter of course or there is mutual violence (each partner initiating violence and maintaining a similar level of power in the relationship), the violence escalates more quickly than it does among couples in which just one person uses violence, making serious injuries or death more likely to occur.

6. DON'T TRY TO MANIPULATE A BATTERER. You can't outmanipulate a manipulator. To be effective, you must play on your own field, not his. In her phone conversation with Mike, Jackie was, in a sense, trying to manipulate him into believing her story about why Beth refused to come to the phone. She was trying, through her lies, to stay on Mike's good side in the hope that she, Diane, and Beth would be better off for it. What is ironic is that he saw right through her lies, and thought worse of her than before the conversation. Her attempt to manipulate him backfired.

7. IF YOU REINFORCE A BATTERER'S ABUSIVE BEHAVIORS BY GIVING HIM WHAT HE WANTS WHEN HE IS ABUSIVE, HE WILL CONTINUE TO BEHAVE THAT WAY. It is the same principle as with parenting children, but it becomes potentially lethal when you are dealing with a violent adult. If he calls to tell you that he will slit the tires on your car if you don't tell him where his wife and children are, don't tell him where they are. That won't keep him from vandalizing your car. Do something which is more likely to work (e.g., call the police and report his threat, move your car inside a locked garage, etc.).

If he stands in your front yard with a gun to his head, saying he'll shoot himself if you don't talk to him about his girlfriend, don't do it. Call the police and report his suicidal threat. Don't feel like you have to appease him or be controlled by him in order to keep yourself or anyone else safe. Indeed, if he believes that you are easily controlled, he is *more* likely to threaten you—unless, of course, you are willing to give up your helpful role with your battered woman. He'd like that.

8. SET YOUR OWN LIMITS AND CONSE-QUENCES TO HIS BEHAVIOR, AND FOLLOW THROUGH. The safest thing for you to do in most circumstances is to find real consequences (which will cause him discomfort) to his abusive behavior toward you and follow through with them consistently. For example, if you have decided to call the police when he comes to your door, you must call them *every* time, no matter what the police do or say—you may have to advocate for yourself with higher-ups in the department if the officers aren't co-operative in your efforts to stay safe.

Batterers let their partners know in no uncertain terms that they will hurt them worse or kill them should they call the police or "get them in trouble." Most battered women I have counseled are initially terrified to file assault com-plaints, protective orders, or anything else which their abusive partners won't like. Many women eventually come to recognize, however, that they are in danger either way; they are being hurt even when they are appeasing their partner's every wish. Many of these women eventually de-cide that having a protective order, for instance, is better than having nothing. Though some batterers ignore court orders or other such threats of disciplinary action, many will discontinue (at least temporarily) their violent behav-ior when they see that punishment for that behavior is un-comfortable and inevitable.

The guy who battered me stalked me for about one year after he beat me up. During that year, even though I had a

Peace Bond against him (which the judge later informed me wasn't worth the paper it was written on), Joe managed to threaten and harass me with frightening regularity. One time he called to let me know he had found out my un-listed telephone number. Another time he showed up outside my work and stood in front of my car so I would be forced to talk to him (he was terribly surprised and jumped out of the way when I started to run over him!). Terrifying as they were to me, neither of his behaviors were illegal at the time. When he showed up at my apartment one day (after I had been painstakingly careful not to disclose the location of it), banging and shaking the doorknob, I called the police and reported that someone was trying to break in. They were able to catch him and arrest him. He never bothered me again.

Laws may exist in your area designed to help you *before* he hurts you. Set up and utilize legal and practical conse-quences to his abusive behaviors. Try to work that out first with the cooperation of his partner, the woman you care about. For example, if she just left him and came to your house for safety, you might speak with her about getting an order of protection so that the police can arrest him should he come knocking on your door. If neither you nor she have a protective order, he may have a legal right to knock at your door (depending on your state's laws regard-ing domestic abuse). He would have to commit a crime (e.g., breaking into your home or hurting someone) before police could arrest him.

Don't in any way force your battered friend or relative to get a protective order or, for that matter, to take any ac-tion to actively protect herself. That would be too control-ling and alienating of her. But, even if she doesn't take action to keep herself safe from him, you should do what

you can to keep yourself, and those people you are responsible for, safe. Be sure to tell her what action you plan to
take. Places which might offer help:

- Your police department, district attorney's office, or battered women's shelter organization can tell you about
  orders of protection and laws in your area regarding domestic abuse. They might also offer information concerning what type of police response you can expect on
  domestic violence–related calls where you live. This can
  vary widely from jurisdiction to jurisdiction. You may
  need to know, for example, how police tend to respond
  if you call with a frantic plea for help because your
  daughter's abusive boyfriend just called to say that he
  was coming over to "talk" to your daughter and he
  threatened you over the phone five times yesterday.
- The batterer's boss (especially in cases where he is military or police, etc.)—and seek help in the form of job
  sanctions if he bothers you again. I've known of situations where commanding officers and police chiefs have
  told batterers who worked for them that they would
  lose their jobs if they abused their partners again. The
  prospect of losing his job can be a strong deterrent for a
  career military man or police officer. Abused partners of
  these men, however, are usually very hesitant to seek
  job sanctions, fearing loss of income.

9. PLAN AHEAD FOR WHAT ACTION HE MIGHT
TAKE. If you have reason to believe that a batterer might
be dangerous to you, try to stay one step ahead of what he
might be thinking. To help with this you can play the

"what if" game. Ask yourself questions like, "What if he followed me home and stood in front of my door so that I couldn't get in until I talked to him about Joni?" "What would I say if he threatened to hurt me if I didn't tell him where Joni was staying?" Preparing yourself in this way can help you react more quickly and confidently in case a similar scenario does happen.

Be aware that other people may accuse you of being paranoid if you plan ahead in this way. Many people in our society have no experience with the irrational nature of domestic violence. They presume that what happens must be similar to disagreements in nonviolent relationships. So when you plan for the worst and it doesn't appear, many people presume that you are overreacting to the situation. IT IS NEXT TO IMPOSSIBLE TO BE TOO CAUTIOUS WHEN DEALING WITH A VIOLENT PERSON! Paranoia is characterized by an unrealistic fear. If you are afraid of someone who has demonstrated that he has the potential to physically injure and terrorize people, this is a reasonable fear.

Sample Anchor Conversations with Batterers

Anchor: Jack, Ralph mentioned to me that you tore up your house yesterday. (Assertive language)

Jack: Oh yeah, I got a little mad at Sally 'cause she wouldn't deal with the kids and I was studying for my final. They were all screaming and I couldn't concentrate. I ended up slamming down the phone receiver, that's all.

Anchor: I understood from Ralph that you broke a
           chair and lamp and threw stuff around for
           thirty minutes. (Not colluding with him to
           minimize or shift blame)

Jack: What are you doing talking to Ralph about
           my private business anyway?

Anchor: I was just concerned about your family.
           What you did sounded very scary. (Assertive
           language)

Jack: There was nothing scary about it. The kids
           were the ones screaming, not me.

———

Tom: (Phone call to Anchor) I know you know
           where my wife and kids are staying and I
           know that you were the one who told them
           to leave me. It'll be a lot easier on you if you
           tell me where they are.

Anchor: What do you mean easier on me? Are you
           threatening me, Tom? (Trust your instincts)

Tom: Take it as you will. Are you going to tell me
           where they are?

Anchor: No. I'll be reporting your threat to the police
           and I won't be talking to you anymore.
           (Hangs up and keeps hanging up each time
           Tom calls) (Sets consequences and follows
           through)

———

Chris:	Hey Cara, did you hear that Sharon and I got back together?
Anchor:	No. I hadn't heard.
Chris:	Yeah. She forgives me for my hurting her last time and I swore to her that I wouldn't hurt her again.
Anchor:	I'm still angry at you for hurting Sharon, Chris, and while I think you probably *believe* you won't hurt her again, you probably *will* do it again if you don't get counseling for your problem. (Assertive language)
Chris:	I managed to stop drinking without counseling and I can do this, too. Besides, we love each other and that's what really matters. We can work out any problem if we love each other enough.
Anchor:	It isn't a relationship problem. It is *your* problem and you need professional help. (Not colluding with him to shift blame)

WHEN YOU CARE ABOUT THE COUPLE

This book has been written for the perspective of the ally of the battered woman. However, the advice contained in it can also be applied to situations in which other forms of alliances exist. You may care deeply about both partners of a couple but have learned that one of them is physically abusing the other. To care about them both equally (or the batterer above the battered woman) puts you in a very difficult position. To act as anchor for her would tend to alienate you from him. On the other hand, to be a confidante for him might put you in a position of knowing the danger in her situation, but being unable to help her.

You might also find yourself in the uncomfortable position of mediator, acting to help them talk out their problems reasonably. This is akin to acting as counselor to your battered friend or relative and I caution you against taking a mediator role. Not only is it physically dangerous for you, but it's practically impossible to accomplish anything of benefit to anyone in the mediator role because of your relationship to them. Leave that role to skilled professionals who have no previous personal relationship to the people involved. Everyone will be better off for it.

There are ways to stay involved with a couple without being either distant or overinvolved, just as with an abused woman. Below, I've listed a few principles which may help you negotiate this difficult circumstance. You'll notice that they are similar to principles discussed previously, though they encourage you to express your beliefs and opinions more boldly than you might if you were beginning to work on a stronger connection with an abused woman alone:

1. Do not underestimate the power of a family secret like partner abuse. It is so powerful that you can expect there to be a great deal of pressure on you to keep the secret. If you decide to act as anchor and speak about it openly, being the one to disclose the secret, you may meet with resistance, hostility, or resentment from those involved in keeping the secret (abused woman and batterer alike).

2. Always keep in mind: violent relationships are usually not as they seem. Accept that there are probably parts of their relationship that you will never know about or completely understand. You can be an anchor without complete knowledge or understanding.

3. Be clear about any behavior which you don't like, e.g., "You are both my friends, but I believe his use of violence is wrong."

4. Don't minimize how dangerous his use of violence is. To do so doesn't help either party. "Sally, I like Jack but I'm very scared for you when he gets violent." "Jack, your violence scares me and I'm afraid for Sally's life when you get violent."

5. Don't suggest or imply that his abuse is in any way her fault or that she can do something to change it. "Jack, nothing she did justifies your hitting her." "Sally, you can't *make* someone hit you. So nothing you do can *make* him stop hitting you."

6. Don't accept his excuses for his behavior. Let him know that you think he needs professional help. "Jack, lots of people lose their jobs. That doesn't make it O.K. for them to beat their wives. You need special professional counseling to help you stop abusing her."

ABOUT HELP FOR BATTERERS

MEN WHO ABUSE THEIR PARTNERS ALMOST NEVER BECOME LESS VIOLENT OR ABUSIVE

WITHOUT PROFESSIONAL HELP *SPECIFICALLY GEARED FOR THEM*, even though many of them would like to think that they can. Indeed, as the cycle indicates in Chapter Three, a batterer's abuse usually gets worse over the course of a relationship, not better. Even when batterers do go to counseling, their abusive tendencies may be overlooked by their counselors/therapists because they often look quite normal psychologically. Such an experience is extremely demoralizing to the victim of his abuse and can cause her to doubt her own judgment. "If this therapist doesn't think he's abusive, maybe I really am blowing this out of proportion like my partner has been claiming all along."

Even when a counselor knows that a client is physically abusive, he or she may not be educated as to the appropriate treatment for him. Several men with whom I am familiar have gone into therapy to help them stop their physical and emotional abuse of their partner and their therapists have done communication skills training and even regression work due to the abuse they suffered as children. Meanwhile, their ability to handle their anger in nonabusive, nonviolent ways were not directly addressed and therefore did not significantly improve.

It has been my experience that most batterers neither stay in specialized therapy long enough nor do the kind of work necessary to get significantly better over the long term. This is not to say that with the proper help there is no chance that a particular batterer will get better. It is to say that you should not be deluded into thinking that just because an abusive man you know has gone to a therapist once a week for two months that he is no longer a danger to you or his partner.

If you suspect that a batterer is mentally ill and a danger to himself or others, you may be able to call the police to have him placed in protective custody (and involuntarily committed for assessment at a mental hospital). Although laws about when the police can or will intervene in a situation like this differ from state to state, you can always call your local police or mental health association and ask about procedures in your area.

If you believe a batterer has a substance abuse problem, but isn't showing that he is an immediate threat to himself or those around him (so that you can call and report him to police), you can either stay away from him, get an order of protection, and/or recommend to him that he seek professional help for his substance abuse and violence. Be especially safety-conscious around batterers who abuse substances as they are usually extremely unpredictable and particularly volatile.

ANSWERS TO QUESTIONS YOU MIGHT HAVE

Won't it just make him madder if I don't do what he wants?

Most people are afraid to use these methods believing that it will only make a batterer more angry and violent. And yes, to use these methods might make him angrier, although probably not more violent.

Batterers set people up to worry about their reactions. Since he doesn't want to pay the dues for his misdeeds, a batterer will usually scare people into believing that if they don't do what he wants or if they hold him accountable for his violent actions, he will hurt someone or break something of theirs (e.g., car, house windows, other property). This is often a bluff; his smoke screen.

Having a protective order does not mean that you can let your guard down. No one can give you any guarantees about a batterer's behavior. He may hurt you if you don't do what he wants you to do. He may hurt you if you do exactly what he wants. The point is, you can't control what he does. You are, however, going to be in a safer position with the average batterer if you use the methods listed here than if you don't.

Aren't some women just as physically abusive to their husbands as their husbands are to them?

Yes. True mutual violence in relationships happens, but accurate statistics telling us how often it happens are very difficult to get. It happens in a very small percentage of the domestic violence cases I see. Battered women do sometimes fight back, as I explained in Chapter Seven, yet a distinction should be made between fighting back and mutual violence. True mutual violence involves two people who vie for power in their relationship using basically equivalent strategies and with similar results. They each intimidate and scare the other equally. One person is not generally more afraid of the other.

When battered women fight back, however, they are usually attempting to gain some semblance of power and control in a relationship where they have very little. But fighting back doesn't work as hoped to regain that control and power. Indeed, it usually backfires, with the batterer taking more control than ever, a dynamic that most battered women learn quickly before discarding the fighting-back strategy.

CHAPTER NINE

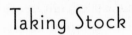

Taking Stock

Having read up to this point, how do you feel? Overwhelmed, excited, sorry, guilty, rejuvenated, pensive? You probably still don't *feel* like an anchor yet, even though you may be *behaving* like one some of the time. The feeling of being an anchor will come in its own time, with your patience and hard work. Anchor can become a permanent part of yourself, a set of tools you can pull out and use when you want or need to help someone.

WHERE ARE JACKIE, KATE, AND DIANE?

Jackie has come a long way from her distant judgment of battered women as spineless wimps to the awareness of herself as a connected, vulnerable human being—an anchor.

Before Jackie and her sister Kate realized there was work to be done within their relationships with Diane, they sat on opposite ends of the same ship—they both loved Diane and were concerned about her living with an abusive husband, but had very different ways of showing their concern. Jackie tended to emotionally remove herself, remaining uninvolved, at least on the surface. Through her demeanor, she was inadvertently sending Diane the message, "I don't care enough to be more involved with you." Kate's well-meaning attempts to control aspects of Diane's life kept her overinvolved. Kate's implied message: "Stay with me, *little* sister. You need me to solve your problems for you." Neither way was right or wrong. Also, neither way worked to show Diane the true nature of their concern.

Though it happened at different times for them, both Jackie and Kate accepted the challenge to work toward relationships with Diane (and subsequently others) that would be based on mutual respect and care. Jackie had to step closer to Diane, Kate had to step back. Their stories illustrate that the path toward becoming an anchor may be very different for each person, even within the same family.

Kate has worked on her tendency to rescue people she cares about most and is making good progress, though she often fails to recognize her improvement amid everyday struggles.

For Jackie, the key element in becoming an anchor was her acknowledgment that she could change the nature of her relationships by changing the way she behaved within them. She began by making changes in the way she behaved within her more comfortable friendships, being more open with friends about problems in her life. She was surprised when this actually worked—they started entrusting their own stories to her, which opened up discussions of a more personal sort than she had ever imagined possible. With this as reinforcement Jackie forged ahead, allowing herself to be more vulnerable so as not to come across as the judgmental know-it-all she had once appeared to be. Friends not only shared their problems with her, they actually started seeking out her support. Her relationships began to deepen in inexplicable ways. At the same time, she was utilizing her new skills within her relationship with Diane with hope that closeness would develop between them. More recently, Jackie has been working on changing how she conducts herself with other family members so that those relationships can be deepened, too. She has already begun reaping the rewards of that effort.

It is important to note that Jackie still has to think about her reactions to some difficult situations. She still reviews even the most basic communication skills as she notices herself needing to use them. But she is much more comfortable with her new way of handling relationships today than she ever dreamed she'd be when she undertook the process of change, two years ago.

Happily, Diane is alive and well. She can still cry at the thought of what she went through at the hands of her husband and in relief that she and their daughter got away safely. She remembers the night she made that final decision to leave Mike:

We were going to move, yet again, the next day. I had been dreading another move, knowing that it would take me to a remote area where I would have no friends and have to start all over again at a new job. Nicole Brown Simpson had just been murdered and that was also weighing heavily on my mind. Most important,

Beth had been complaining for a few weeks that her father had been hurting her. I didn't want to believe it, but I did.

We were all packed when Mike started abusing me. He kept me up all night, as usual, forcing me to listen as he ranted and raved about who knows what. All I could think about while he was abusing me was how I was going to leave him in the morning. Just make it through this one, I told myself, and tomorrow Beth and I are gone for good. The next morning finally came and Mike went to work, thinking we would meet him that evening at our new home. Immediately after he closed the door I ran to the phone to call Jackie. We had been talking over the phone regularly for several months and she was the only one I felt comfortable asking for help.

When I reached Jackie she was calm and rational, but clearly relieved that I was leaving my husband. My adrenaline was working overtime and I was having trouble concentrating. I kept asking Jackie how I was going to get our clothes (they were already at the new house). She reasoned with me and helped me think about our safety first. She also said we could stay with her, so we jumped into the car with nothing but the clothes on our backs and drove the ten hours to Jackie's house and my hometown. I don't remember much about the days after I arrived at Jackie's house. I just focused on making it through and finding my daughter the therapeutic help she needed after her father's abuse. Jackie gave me space and listened when I needed to talk, but each day she grew more nervous about the possibility that Mike would come looking for us. For her family's safety and ours she suggested that we move to another location, a place Mike didn't know. That was hard for me to hear at the time, but I understood and agreed. My parents helped me find a new place and I've been here ever since. It was very hard at first, struggling financially, handling my daughter's behavior, being lonely. But I made it. I'm successful at my job. I'm closer to Jackie than ever before. Kate and I still like each other though we are not as close as we used to be. But, that's good. We were too close before. Beth still has some struggles as a result of the abuse she suffered, but she is improving.

Jackie and Diane's relationship continues to progress and has developed a mutuality of care and support, with Diane calling Jackie, being there for her, initiating a connection with her. But Jackie still finds it necessary to remind herself that she wants a good, open relationship with Diane regardless of what Diane does and whom she chooses to date or marry. Jackie has had to face up to her own expectations and hidden agendas. She has come to realize that to love Diane means to accept her for who she is, not for who she should be.

An integral part of Jackie's progress was developing her ability to observe her own behavior more objectively. In practicing this new self-awareness, Jackie recently came to some disturbing insights concerning her own anger and need for control within close relationships. Similarly, other people I have known (including myself), in their work with and around violent families, have had to come to terms with their own aggressive or passive tendencies. So when Jackie told me that she was concerned that she was too aggressive and domineering toward those people she loves most, I responded: "Congratulations!" I told her that I saw it as a testament to her hard work. She wouldn't have been at that point had she only just begun the process of becoming someone's anchor. She has come to the realization that she's not omnipotent or so different from Diane, or any other battered woman, batterer, or violent couple. It is a very healthy step in becoming an anchor to recognize that you are human with human faults and frailties. The important thing is that Jackie is using the information she has acquired about herself toward a positive end. Just noticing her overly controlling or aggressive tendencies is working on it.

Jackie listened to me, reluctant to share my enthusiasm. "Another thing to work on," she sighed, knowing that excitement and fear lay ahead. But, once again, she bravely accepted the challenge to change over staying the same. That is the nature of an anchor.

AS FOR ME

It has been thirteen years since I was battered by Joe. I feel fortunate to have lived through and to have learned a lot from my abuse experience, at an age at which I had a lot to learn!

My experience taught me to trust my own instincts and listen to what my head tells me. I learned that there are some situations that are so dangerous or complicated, I need help to handle them well. I also came to appreciate that those people who were there to help me at my lowest point emotionally were the ones I really cared for. The feelings I had for my boyfriend were based on fun and excitement, not care and respect. I learned what to look for to find a mutually respectful, mature relationship. I found just that and have been happily married for ten years and have two beautiful children.

The experience also made me more humble and understanding of other people's difficulties. It spawned my interest in helping other battered women and their family members and friends, an interest I've been pursuing since my ordeal.

Along the way, I have been fortunate to get to know many fine people, including friends, clients, and colleagues, who share a common interest: to make our world a safer, more peaceful place in which to live. That is the kind of world I hope to hand down to my children.

HOW TO KNOW WHEN YOU'VE BECOME AN ANCHOR

As I've discussed before, you can *act* like an anchor before being an anchor. But how do you know when you actually *are* an anchor for a particular woman? The answer to that is surprisingly simple: when she trusts and accepts you for the help and support you provide. Perhaps she calls you regularly to find someone who will understand. Perhaps she relies on your support when she feels particularly overwhelmed or sad. Perhaps she calls on you to accompany her to appearances at the courthouse. Perhaps she comes to you when she needs a place to stay or someone to pick her up after an incident. Perhaps she calls you just to chat. Having an anchor means different things to different women. You'll probably know when you're playing that role in a woman's life by the strong sense of connectedness you feel when you are with her.

How do you know when you have the ability, in general, to be an anchor? When anchor skills are becoming second nature to you. You will know when you have developed those skills to a comfortable and efficacious point when:

1. You have a sense that a friend, relative, or acquaintance might be in an abusive relationship and you pay attention to that sense.

2. You know how to establish contact and trust with her.

3. You recognize when she is dropping clues to her abuse story.

4. You know how to respond effectively when she drops clues to her abuse.

5. You are aware of your own reactions, feelings, and needs with regard to her abuse and your relationship with her.

6. You no longer try to change her when you disagree with her decisions or actions (or lack thereof).

7. You know how to respond effectively when she shares her story of abuse with you or comes to you directly for help.

8. You are able to make conscious decisions about what kind of help you can provide and what role you can play in her life.

9. You are confident in your ability to find out how best to help her if you are unsure.

10. You are able to be assertive and aware with regard to her abusive partner.

WHEN AM I DONE?

Never. There will always be opportunities to be an anchor for someone and you will probably always have to review and polish your anchor skills from time to time. People tend to not use their anchor tools often enough to keep them from getting rusty. But once they are there in your tool box, anchor skills are relatively easy to polish.

HOW JACKIE FEELS ABOUT BEING AN ANCHOR

I remember the first time my anchor skills worked. I was talking to a friend and she mentioned that her father was an alcoholic. Immediately, a siren went off in my head alerting me that she might be dropping a clue to a bigger story. I had been learning about the characteristics of batterers and knew that often alcoholics were also abusive, so I cautiously asked if he had ever abused her. To my surprise, she answered "yes," and for the next two hours she told me the story of her father's abuse of her. I couldn't believe our conversation was going so well. It was because *I* was being very different. I was asking open-ended questions so she could control her end of the conversation, and I was really listening and clarifying what I didn't understand. I was acting like an anchor! I had known my friend ten years and until that day had not been particularly close to her. That day changed all that.

From time to time I think back three years ago when I started this journey toward becoming an anchor and I can't believe I'm the same person. I shudder to think how distant and removed I was from people. I had no compassion for myself, let alone others. I was ignorant about physical and emotional abuse. Indeed, I didn't think I knew anyone in that situation.

When I look back to the opinion I had of my sister Diane in those days I am saddened and embarrassed. I had forgotten how much I cared about her. I didn't even think of her as abused. I thought she and her husband just had "communication problems," and that if she was too weak-willed to stand up for herself and stupid enough to believe her husband's false promises that she deserved him.

On the other hand, it has always been important to me to feel that I could make a difference in the world. That was always easy for me to do in the workplace, everything there was so tangible. But making a difference in another adult's personal life, that was so elusive, reserved for the clergy, therapists, and especially gifted individuals. I didn't think I had it in me.

It turns out I did have it in me, and I have worked hard for a long time to feel this way. Now anchor skills are second nature to me most of the time. I know it's second nature when in a casual conversation someone drops a hint about a "secret." I hear them right away and know how to respond. It feels good to make it easy for someone to get their pain out in the open. Indeed, it can be very exhilarating when things go well; when my sister comes to me for support in a way that she has not sought me out before, when my friend calls me for help with a problem and I'm able to help her feel good about her decisions, when another friend calls to report her own progress because she knew I would appreciate it.

Indeed, it can feel so exhilarating that sometimes I take too much responsibility for other's changes. I can begin to feel the burden of their problems; if I don't call her today will she fall apart or return to her batterer? I can also feel the burden of their successes; if I don't do exactly the "right" thing, will her success continue? Then I have to remind myself that I can't change them or control their outcome. I can only focus on what *I* can do.

Being an anchor has become so natural for me that I'm caught off guard when it doesn't work. Just when I thought I was getting so good at it I am reminded that my tools can get rusty and I need to review the Principles. It can be draining work and sometimes I have to take a break, or better yet call one of *my* anchors. But even though I occasionally forget to use my "tools," I know I can never go back to the way I was before learning them.

What has been most satisfying to me are the changes I see in my own personal relationships with my husband, children, family, and friends. I now know what to do to get closer to those people I care for the most. It feels good to be able to control my actions and responses rather than just saying whatever comes to mind. And to witness the impact that my taking control over myself has on those people around me. It used to feel risky to be open and vulnerable with others. I'm no longer afraid to hear someone's "secrets" and to share my own. Having been relieved of the fear, I'm more at peace.

I thank God for giving me the patience, perseverance, and compassion to become an anchor. I'm grateful that I could face my fears, look within myself, and become a more caring person. I stepped off the sidelines and got involved. I'm proud that, by becoming an anchor for Diane, I had a positive impact on her life.

NOW WHAT DO YOU DO?

As I said in the beginning, I hope you will now put the book down for awhile and sit with what you have read. Trust that you will have a sense of when it is time to pick it up again to reread the parts you will need. In the interim, your mind will be working on becoming an anchor at a subconscious level, and when you are ready to pick it up again, your mind will be primed to *think* about anchor work.

By taking the time and effort to read this book, you have already given your abused friend or relative a loving gift, the gift of compassion. By becoming an anchor you can make your life fuller and more satisfying than you ever imagined. That is a gift only you can give to yourself.

APPENDIX I

—∞∞—

Advocacy

It can be extremely frustrating to work hard toward being an anchor for a battered woman, while at the same time watching her face seemingly insurmountable obstacles within the domestic violence system (courts, police, other institutions). Laws and procedures have changed a lot since the first battered women's shelter was opened twenty-three years ago, making real help for battered women (e.g., safe shelter, "pro-arrest" police policies, protective orders, stalking laws) much more available; however, those systems can still be complicated, intimidating, and lacking.

An advocate can help a woman negotiate the problems she might face in dealing with the domestic violence system. It can be as simple as taking pictures of her bruises, or finding out who she can speak to in the district attorney's office to help her file for a protective order. It can be as complicated as helping her to file complaints against police officers who mishandled her case, or speaking to a judge who isn't taking her situation seriously. If you do advocate for a woman always remember, a good advocate, like a good anchor, lets the woman who is battered direct the effort.

Being an energetic advocate for one woman who is battered not only helps her, it positively impacts the whole domestic violence service system and therefore other battered women. Many women who have been battered come into that system (police, courts, social services, etc.) weary, lacking the kind of energy needed to confront the injustices and prejudices which abound. I've seen women drop complaints of assault simply because they were too intimidated by the criminal justice system to follow through. It's very frightening to appear in court under any circumstances, but even more so if you have to face your batterer there.

What adds to the problem is that every time a woman drops charges against her assaultive partner, some people within the criminal justice system feel reinforced in their stereotypes of battered women: "They all drop charges anyway. Why do we even try to help them if they won't help themselves?" An advocate can bring an essential kind of passion to the effort, the kind of stern resolve to see that things are done properly and with consideration of the victim's needs. Significant change in the system is often the end result.

IDEAS FOR ADVOCACY

1. Accompany her to police departments, court, meetings with lawyers, or wherever else she might feel intimidated or afraid for her safety from him (keep in mind safety issues).

2. Call friends in influential positions to get things done which might help her. My brother knew a man within the state's criminal justice system who pulled some strings so that Joe would be arrested on the assault charges when he appeared at the Peace Bond hearing I requested. (The sheriff's department in the small town where he beat me up couldn't seem to find him at home to arrest him!)

3. Ask her if you can take pictures of her visible injuries after an assault so that she might have evidence of her abuse for any future legal proceedings. For the same reason you might also keep a diary listing dates and pertinent details of assaults she endures.

APPENDIX II

⟨⟨⟨⟩⟩⟩

To Find Good
Professional Help

The idea of going to a therapist or counselor for help makes most people cringe. Excuses not to go abound—I can't afford it, don't have time, don't believe in that touchy-feely stuff, she's the one with the problem, not me, what can a therapist do for me that I can't do for myself? Only you can answer for yourself if your reasons for seeking professional counseling outweigh your reasons not to. It might comfort you to know that thousands of "normal" people seek help in the form of counseling/therapy every day in this country. It doesn't mean they are sick or weak, it just means that they want help from a person who is trained to provide that help.

COUNSELING/THERAPY FOR YOU

If you want professional help for yourself concerning issues related to the abuse of your battered friend or relative (i.e., your role in her life), you can get a referral to an appropriately trained professional several ways. One way is to call the Battered Women's Shelter Organization in your area (or the National Domestic Violence Hotline at 1-800-799-SAFE or TDD at 1-800-787-3224 for help finding the shelter in your area). Shelter Organizations usually know of therapists/counselors they can recommend to people in your position. Social workers at mental health clinics or other social service agencies also often keep abreast of possible referrals for domestic violence–related counseling.

If you have other individual concerns which have surfaced since working toward becoming an anchor for someone, but aren't necessarily directly related to a battered woman (e.g., ability to connect emotionally, assertiveness or communication skills), you might be able to benefit from a therapist/counselor who is more of a general practitioner. For these referrals you can call your medical insurance referral line, area help lines (listed in your phone book), friends who have been in therapy themselves, your family doctor, or area mental health clinic.

WHAT TO ASK, WHAT TO SAY

Nowadays there are people with many different credentials who are licensed and professionally trained to provide psychotherapeutic services. To begin determining whether a therapist/counselor is right for you (let the battered woman do this screening for herself) ask plenty of questions over the phone or at the first visit: How much and what type of experience have you had working with situations like mine? What is your theoretical perspective? How much do you charge per session? Does my medical insurance cover your services? Would I be seen individually or in a group? How many sessions might I need? What are your rules about confidentiality? Are you licensed (in conformity with state requirements) to provide therapy/counseling?

If you can't afford to see a private practitioner, there are many good therapists at nonprofit counseling centers who often have a sliding fee scale (meaning the cost per session is determined by your income). Insurance may cover some of your cost for private or nonprofit care.

Be careful to be honest with your therapist/counselor about any pertinent information about you or events in your life, even if it is embarrassing, so that your counselor can know how best to help you. Your records should be kept confidential.

THERAPY/COUNSELING FOR A BATTERED WOMAN

If you are trying to help a battered woman find therapeutic services, you can also call your local Battered Women's Shelter Organization or, if there isn't one in your area, mental health services agency. Be careful not to get overly involved in the process of finding her professional help. She is more likely to make that difficult first appointment to see a therapist/counselor if she herself goes through the process of deciding whom to see and calls to make the appointment herself. You may be of help to her (if she requests it) by going with her to the first appointment.

Jackie found herself becoming overly involved with Diane's attempts to get into psychotherapy. Jackie wanted so badly for Diane to learn from and get past her abusive marriage that she did much of the initial calling to find the name of a therapist for Diane. When she realized how anxious she was to "get Diane into therapy," she backed off and let Diane take the initiative. And Diane did.

WHEN THERE IS PHYSICAL VIOLENCE WITHIN A RELATIONSHIP, THERAPY/COUNSELING MUST PROCEED DIFFERENTLY THAN IF THERE IS NO VIOLENCE. As I've mentioned in previous chapters, many otherwise knowledgeable professional therapists/counselors are not trained or skilled in issues relating to domestic violence. The part that particularly scares me, though, is that they may not know how to determine whether or not a client is experiencing domestic violence and that they should be determining this in the first place. For example, I am familiar with one therapist with a thriving practice in counseling couples who doesn't believe there is violence in any of his clients' relationships. That is statistically impossible since one-sixth of the population of married women in this country are in physically abusive relationships at any given time.[1] The percentage would naturally be even higher among couples in therapy.

For a marital therapist to fail to recognize violence within a couple's relationship can be very dangerous to the victim of the abuse. Issues may be brought out in the therapy/counseling session which could be used later by the batterer to hurt his partner. In contrast, a therapist who knows how to work with violent couples identifies and deals with the violence first. Other relationship issues exist, of course, but are not the primary focus until the violence is no longer a threat.

[1] M. Straus and R. J. Gelles, "Societal Change and Family Violence from 1975 to 1985 as Revealed by Two National Surveys," *Journal of Marriage and the Family* 48 (1986): 465–79.

APPENDIX III

———⊗⊗⊗———

When the Battered Woman You Care About Is Emotionally Ill

Any woman can find herself dating or otherwise intimately involved with a guy who has the potential to batter her. Many women are emotionally stable before their abusive relationships begin. For some of those women the experience of being in a violent relationship gradually weakens that stability. Other battered women have emotional difficulties (or the tendency toward emotional illness) which existed before the abuse began. For those women, an abusive relationship can worsen their existing illness or be the catalyst for a new episode of illness.

Both depression and anxiety disorders are common among women whose primary love relationship is abusive. Many women at one point or another during their relationship with a batterer even consider suicide as a viable solution to their difficulties. This book is not intended to advise you about situations concerning a friend or relative who has a significant mental or emotional disturbance and who is also battered.

Signs which indicate that your friend or relative needs professional attention:

1. She has a "flat affect"—her expression is dulled and there is no brightness, like flat paint.

2. She cries easily, at things which didn't use to affect her so strongly.

3. She is not interested in usual activities.

4. She has feelings of worthlessness.

5. She sleeps more or less than usual.

6. She loses or gains significant amounts of weight without meaning to.

7. She limits her daily functioning due to a seemingly unreasonable fear of certain objects or situations (e.g., fear of driving on the highway).

8. She has panic attacks or a recurrent sense of doom.

9. She has frequent physical complaints for which there are no medical explanations.

If you notice some of these signs in a woman you care about, perhaps you could speak to her about your concerns and encourage her to seek professional help. Since battered women are sometimes misdiagnosed by well-meaning mental health professionals who don't know she's been abused and/or who aren't trained to help battered women, you, as her anchor, may be able to help her find help which is appropriate for her (see Appendix II on finding good professional help).

Signs of distress which would indicate the need for *immediate* professional help include:

1. She talks about committing suicide.

2. She has hallucinations or delusions (seeing or hearing things that aren't there).

3. She is out of touch with reality—doesn't know what day it is, who the president is, or what city she's in.

4. She is highly paranoid—thinks people are out to get her (people other than the batterer).

If your loved one is resistant to seeking professional help herself and you believe she may be mentally ill such that she could be a danger to herself or others, you can consult with a knowledgeable professional yourself. Do so immediately if the threat of danger is imminent. Too many families or friends have lost loved ones to suicide because they hesitated to seek professional assistance; they didn't want to "betray" their loved one or they assumed she would eventually get over it. When in doubt, check it out!

APPENDIX IV

———⚬⚬⚬———

When the Woman You Care About Abuses Alcohol or Drugs

Some battered women abuse alcohol and/or drugs. Some of these women abuse substances because it makes it easier to cope with the cloud of fear and stress under which they live. Also, many batterers strongly encourage or force their partners to drink and drug with them as a way of shifting the focus away from their own abusive behavior, "See how much she drinks? She has more problems than I do." Other battered women are prone to substance abuse problems on their own, without relation to their abusive circumstances.

It is very easy to blame a substance-abusing woman for the abusive circumstances in which she lives. It is also very difficult for a friend or relative to maintain any sort of positive, helpful relationship with that woman by virtue of the way the substance affects her personality and behavior. Indeed, I believe that it is virtually impossible to achieve an anchor relationship with a person who is actively using drugs and/or alcohol.

What *can* you do? Without judging or chastising, you can encourage her into substance abuse treatment. It is best, at the same time, to encourage her into relationship abuse counseling, too (unless there is a counselor in your area who does both well). This way the substance abuse counselor, the relationship abuse counselor, and the woman can determine the best course of treatment for her. I say this because some clients of mine have gone into treatment for their own substance abuse but their counselors were not trained or skilled in dealing with the level of immediate physical danger she was experiencing in her relationship. At the same time, not much real work can be done in relationship abuse counseling when an individual is actively using.

What can you do to encourage her to seek treatment? For specific information answering that question call Alcoholics Anonymous (AA), Al-Anon (for family members of alcohol abusers), Narcotics Anonymous, and/or your local Women's Shelter Organization (they are used to dealing with substance abuse and relationship abuse issues).

————◦◦◦————

Child Abuse
and Neglect

A high percentage of children within families where partner abuse exists are themselves abused or neglected also. If
you have a reasonable suspicion that a child you know of is
or has been physically, emotionally, sexually abused or neglected, you have a duty to see to it that a report of that
abuse if made to the proper authorities. IN MOST AREAS
OF THIS COUNTRY, YOU, AS AN ADULT CITIZEN,
ARE LEGALLY RESPONSIBLE TO REPORT CHILD
ABUSE OF WHICH YOU HAVE KNOWLEDGE.

Just like adult batterers, child abusers usually don't seek
help on their own, and without help they don't usually
stop abusing their children. If they don't stop abusing their
children, those children are scarred, emotionally and sometimes physically, for life. Sometimes they even die at the
hands of their abusive parent! If you find you have a nagging feeling that a child you know is being mistreated,
PAY ATTENTION TO THAT FEELING. Try to gather as

much information about that situation as you can. Think of it this way: if the child you're worried about *is* being abused and you don't help that child, who will?

Following is a list of common signs of child abuse and neglect. Generally speaking, "child abuse" encompasses physical, psychological, or sexual harm done to a child. "Child neglect" usually involves abandonment or lack of proper care. The two terms overlap in some ways, as "harm" and "lack of care" are sometimes difficult to distinguish. State laws, however, in spelling out what is considered abuse or neglect can be quite specific. Just as with signs of partner abuse, the existence of one of these signs of child abuse and neglect does not necessarily mean that a child is being mistreated. The existence of one sign means that the child may be abused or neglected, and you should be on alert for other information or signs which would confirm or negate your suspicions. You can always call the child protective agency in your area to ask questions without necessarily making a report.

Emotional Abuse
- delayed in physical or emotional development
- sleep or eating disorders
- exhibits self-destructive behavior
- uses drugs or alcohol
- extreme mood changes or behavior swings
- destructive, aggressive, or withdrawn

Physical Abuse
- unusual fractures, bruises, or burns
- feels deserving of harsh punishment
- is very aggressive or very withdrawn
- seems afraid of parents or caretakers

- is uncomfortable with physical contact
- has frequent injuries which caretakers say are "accidental"
- wears clothing inappropriate for the weather to hide injuries

Physical Neglect
- continually hungry, emaciated
- lethargic, tired, apathetic, or self-destructive
- has poor hygiene
- clothes are inappropriate for the weather
- home is unsafe or unsanitary
- medical and/or dental needs are not being addressed
- child is not being supervised properly
- assumes adult responsibilities
- poor school attendance, tardiness, drops out

Sexual Abuse
- sexual knowledge or behavior beyond what is considered age appropriate
- torn or stained underpants
- eating disorders
- pain or itch in the genital area
- frequent urinary or vaginal infections
- marked avoidance of certain adults or places
- frequent stress-related somatic complaints (e.g., headaches, stomachaches)
- depression, suicidal gestures or talk, lack of emotional control
- chronic runaway
- pregnancy in young adolescence
- sexually transmitted diseases

ABUSE OF A PREGNANT WOMAN

If you know a pregnant woman who is being physically abused by her partner, be aware that the legal issues surrounding reporting the abuse of the unborn fetus differ from state to state. To find out what the laws are in your state, call the Child Protection Agency or Women's Shelter Organization in your area. Certainly consider discussing your concerns for the safety of her unborn child with the pregnant mother (using your good communication skills from Chapter Five).

HOW TO REPORT CHILD ABUSE

Call the state Child Protection Agency in your area. Your police department or Family Court office can give you the phone number if you can't find it in your phone book. You can make your report anonymously. The social workers there will ask you questions and decide, from your report, the probable level of danger to the child and whether or not the case should be investigated further. Make a point of getting the name of the caseworker who is taking your report so that he or she can be held accountable for his or her handling of the case. Doing this also gives you a contact person through whom you can check on the case status (within the limits of confidentiality).

APPENDIX VI

Resources

DOMESTIC VIOLENCE

National Coalition Against Domestic Violence
800-799-7233 or 800-787-3224 (TDD)

National Organization for Victim Assistance
800-879-6682

National Resource Center on Domestic Violence
800-537-2238

LEGAL HELP

Your state or local bar association (for referral to an attorney with experience in the area with which you are concerned)

Your local Legal Aid Society or Legal Services (for low-income clients)

MENTAL HEALTH SERVICES

Your family physician (for referral to appropriate services)

Your local center for mental health services (often listed in the phone book under the State Department of Human Services)

Your local Battered Women's Shelter Organization

PROGRAMS FOR ABUSIVE PARENTS

Child Help USA
800-422-4453 (including hearing impaired)

CHILD ABUSE AND NEGLECT

Child Abuse and Neglect Clearinghouse
800-394-3366

National Council on Child Abuse and Family Violence
202-429-6695

Your local authority for reporting child abuse or neglect (often under your State Department of Human Services)

SUBSTANCE ABUSE

Alcoholics Anonymous World Services, Inc.
212-870-3400

Al-Anon World Service Office
800-356-9996

Centers for Substance Abuse Treatments
800-662-4357

National Clearinghouse for Alcohol and Drug Information
800-729-6686 or 877-767-8432 (Spanish)

CHILD SUPPORT ENFORCEMENT

Association for Children for Enforcement of Support
800-537-7072

Your local district attorney's office or
State Department of Human Services

STATE COALITIONS

To get help or give help, call your State Coalition Office to find the
program offering shelter and support nearest to you. Please note that
while these phone numbers were accurate at the time of printing, they
may have changed. An updated list appears on the National Coalition
Against Domestic Violence web site (http://www.ncadv.org).

- Alabama Coalition Against Domestic Violence
     334-832-4842

- Alaska Network on Domestic Violence & Sexual Assault
     907-586-3650

- Arizona Coalition Against Domestic Violence
     602-279-2900

- Arkansas Coalition Against Domestic Violence
     501-812-0571

- California Alliance Against Domestic Violence
     916-444-7163

- Statewide California Coalition for Battered Women
    562-981-1202

- Colorado Coalition Against Domestic Violence
    303-831-9632

- Connecticut Coalition Against Domestic Violence
    860-282-7899

- Delaware Coalition Against Domestic Violence
    302-658-2958

- District of Columbia Coalition Against Domestic Violence
    202-783-5332

- Florida Coalition Against Domestic Violence
    850-425-2749

- Georgia Coalition Against Domestic Violence
    770-984-0085

- Hawaii State Coalition Against Domestic Violence
    808-486-5072

- Idaho Coalition Against Sexual and Domestic Violence
    208-384-0419

- Illinois Coalition Against Domestic Violence
    217-789-2830

- Indiana Coalition Against Domestic Violence
    317-543-3908

- Iowa Coalition Against Domestic Violence
    515-244-8028

- Kansas Coalition Against Sexual & Domestic Violence
    785-232-9784

- Kentucky Domestic Violence Association
    502-695-2444

- Louisiana Coalition Against Domestic Violence
    225-752-1296

- Maine Coalition to End Domestic Violence
    207-941-1194

- Maryland Network Against Domestic Violence
    301-352-4574

- Massachusetts Coalition Against Sexual Assault & Domestic Violence
    617-248-0922

- Michigan Coalition Against Domestic and Sexual Violence
    517-347-7000

- Minnesota Coalition for Battered Women
    651-646-6177

- Mississippi Coalition Against Domestic Violence
    601-981-9196

- Missouri Coalition Against Domestic Violence
    573-634-4161

- Montana Coalition Against Domestic and Sexual Violence
    406-443-7794

- Nebraska Domestic Violence / Sexual Assault Coalition
    402-476-6256

- Nevada Network Against Domestic Violence
    775-828-1115

- New Hampshire Coalition Against Domestic and Sexual Violence
    603-224-8893

- New Jersey Coalition for Battered Women
    609-584-8107

- New Mexico Coalition Against Domestic Violence
    505-246-9240

- New York State Coalition Against Domestic Violence
    518-432-4864

- North Carolina Coalition Against Domestic Violence
    919-956-9124

- North Dakota Council on Abused Women's Services
    701-255-6240

- Ohio Domestic Violence Network
    614-784-0023

- Action Ohio Coalition for Battered Women
    614-221-1255

- Oklahoma Coalition Against Domestic Violence & Sexual Assault
    405-848-1815

- Oregon Coalition Against Domestic and Sexual Violence
    503-365-9644

- Pennsylvania Coalition Against Domestic Violence
    717-545-6400

- Comisión Para los Asuntos de la Mujer, Puerto Rico
    787-722-2907

- Rhode Island Coalition Against Domestic Violence
    401-467-9940

- South Carolina Coalition Against Domestic Violence & Sexual Assault
    803-256-2900

- South Dakota Coalition Against Domestic Violence & Sexual Assault
      605-945-0869

- Tennessee Task Force Against Domestic Violence
      615-386-9406

- Texas Council on Family Violence
      512-794-1133

- Utah Domestic Violence Advisory Council
      801-538-9886

- Vermont Network Against Domestic Violence and Sexual Assault
      802-223-1302

- Virginians Against Domestic Violence
      757-221-0990

- Washington State Coalition Against Domestic Violence
      360-407-0756

- West Virginia Coalition Against Domestic Violence
      304-965-3552

- Wisconsin Coalition Against Domestic Violence
      608-255-0539

- Wyoming Coalition Against Domestic Violence and Sexual Assault
      307-755-5481

- Women's Resource Center, Virgin Islands
      340-773-9272

- Women's Coalition of St. Croix, Virgin Islands
      340-773-9272

ACKNOWLEDGMENTS

Writing this book has been a very personal process for me. As such, there are many people who have supported and influenced me and this work. My friend and favorite poet, Linda Pessolano Swindle, used her talents to edit the work from its inception. Another friend, Patti Weiser, bolstered me with her relentless enthusiasm while helping me organize and conceptualize this book.

I want to thank my husband, Jim, for his unassuming, constant support of me throughout this project; my brother Doug and life-long friend Vicki, for believing in me all along; my parents, Lyle and Marie, and my other brothers, L.G. and Bob, for always being there when I need them.

Thanks also to Donna Pope, M.S.W., for being my comrade and mentor and for giving me the opportunity to work with abuse survivors. I'm also grateful to Abbey Meyering, PH.D., and Julia Dodson, M.S.W., for helping me better understand the dynamics of domestic violence. Thanks to the women in my Mom's Etc. Group for helping me stay sane and productive through these last "childbearing" years. Finally, thanks to all the clients, friends, and acquaintances who have trusted me with their stories. You've given me more than you'll ever know.

ABOUT THE AUTHOR

Susan Brewster has been a clinical social worker/psychotherapist for nineteen years, ten of which have been devoted to working specifically in the area of domestic violence. She has served as clinical director at a battered women's shelter and as a therapist with abused women, their partners and children at a counseling center for violent families. Brewster currently facilitates a support group for the friends and families of abused women and conducts workshops and seminars on issues surrounding domestic violence. She lives with her husband and two children in New Mexico, where she is in private practice.

SELECTED TITLES FROM SEAL PRESS

Getting Free: You Can End Abuse and Take Back Your Life by Ginny NiCarthy, M.S.W. $14.95, 1-878067-92-3. Written by an experienced counselor, this important self-help book provides exercises and practical advice for women who want to break free from abusive relationships.

You Can Be Free: An Easy-to-Read Handbook for Abused Women by Ginny NiCarthy, M.S.W., and Sue Davidson. $10.95, 1-878067-06-0. Written in an accessible style for the woman in crisis, this handbook covers a range of topics designed to help women leave abusive relationships.

A Woman Like You: The Face of Domestic Violence by Vera Anderson. $16.00, 1-878067-07-9. A profoundly inspiring photo-essay book about women who escaped domestic abuse and rebuilt their lives.

Dating Violence: Young Women in Danger edited by Barrie Levy, M.S.W. $18.95, 1-58005-001-8. Written for counselors, social workers and parents, the second edition of this comprehensive resource includes stories from teens in abusive relationships, information from researchers and perspectives from activists who are working in schools and communities.

In Love and In Danger: A Teen's Guide to Breaking Free of Abusive Relationships by Barrie Levy, M.S.W. $10.95, 1-58005-002-6. The second edition of this indispensable guide speaks to teens about what constitutes abusive relationships and how to break free of them. This book gives teens the tools to build healthy relationships and take control of their lives.

New Beginnings: A Creative Writing Guide for Women Who Have Left Abusive Partners by Sharon Doane. $10.95, 1-878067-78-8. An empowering, encouraging book that provides a framework for dealing with the aftermath of an abusive relationship as well as concrete steps to help women discover their creativity and achieve their life goals.

Talking It Out: A Guide to Groups for Abused Women by Ginny NiCarthy, Karen Merriam and Sandra Coffman. $12.95, 0-931188-24-5. Whether you're a counselor, mental health worker or shelter or community activist, *Talking It Out* can help you become more effective in working with women in abusive relationships.

Naming the Violence: Speaking Out About Lesbian Battering edited by Kerry Lobel. $12.95, 0-931188-42-3. For every lesbian battered in an intimate relationship, for every lesbian who has left her lover because of abuse or who wants to, this anthology offers personal stories of pain and empowerment, grief and healing.

Chain Chain Change: For Black Women in Abusive Relationships by Evelyn C. White. $8.95, 1-878067-60-5. Offering supportive, practical information for African-American women who are or have been in a physically or emotionally abusive relationship, this book can help empower women to reclaim a healthier and happier life.

A Community Secret: For the Filipina in an Abusive Relationship by Jacqueline Agtuca. $5.95, 1-878067-44-3. Written in the words of Filipinas who know what it's like to be hurt by the ones they love, this book includes information and supportive advice for women in abusive relationships.

Mommy and Daddy Are Fighting by Susan Paris, illustrated by Gail Labinski. $8.95, 0-931188-33-4. Written from a child's perspective, this gentle and supportive illustrated book tells about the confusing experience of living in a violent home. For ages 4–8.

Mejor Sola Que Mal Acompañada: For the Latina in an Abusive Relationship/Para la Mujer Golpeada by Myrna M. Zambrano. $12.95, 0-931188-26-1. This book offers support, understanding and practical information to Latinas involved in a physically or emotionally abusive relationship.

¡No Más! Guía Para la Mujer Golpeada by Myrna M. Zambrano. $6.95, 1-878067-50-8. A valuable handbook written entirely in Spanish for the Latina in an abusive relationship. Written in simple language that is clear and easy to read, it speaks directly to the Latina in a crisis situation and those who work with her.

Jóvenes, Enamorados y en Peligro: Una guía para los adolescentes para librarse de una relación abusiva by Barrie Levy, M.S.W., and the Los Angeles Commission on Assaults Against Women. $10.95, 1-58005-027-1. This Spanish-language edition of *In Love and In Danger* speaks directly to Latina teens about what constitutes abusive relationships and how to break free of them.

SEAL PRESS publishes many books of fiction and nonfiction by women writers. If you are unable to obtain a Seal Press title from a bookstore or would like a free catalog of our books, please order from us directly by calling 800-754-0271. Visit our web site at www.sealpress.com.